Patty's Poems

by

Patricia Grindel

Proctor Publications, LLC • Ann Arbor • Michigan • USA

Proctor Publications
P.O. Box 2498
Ann Arbor, MI 48106
(800) 343–3034

Publisher's Cataloging in Publication
(Provided by Quality Books, Inc.)

Grindel, Patricia.
    Patty's poems / Patricia Grindel. -- 1st ed.
    p. cm.
    Preassigned LCCN: 98-66621
    ISBN: 1-882792-68-8

    1. Family--Poetry. 2. Friendship--Poetry. 3. Seasons
--Poetry.   I. Title

PS3557.R52P38 1998   811'.54
                                    QBI98-871

Cover design inspired by Meghan Stanbaugh

Printed in the USA

DEDICATION

First of all, I want to thank the Lord I love
 This talent is a gift that comes from above
He blessed me with the most wonderful memory
 When I sit to write, He gives me the ability

This book is dedicated to my late husband, Mel
 The first verse was written for his funeral
People liked it and I got requests for copies
 And you'll find Mel in many of my ditties

I'd also like to make a special dedication
 To family and friends for their inspiration
They took me at face value and said I could
 If I could, then I should and sure would

I also wish to thank all those great folks
 Who gave me their life stories for my prose
For they helped to make this book what it is
 And I learned a lot about them doing this

Patricia Hrindel

February 26th, 1997

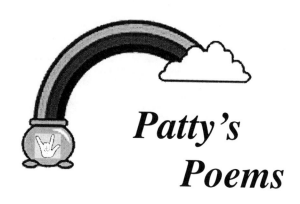

Patty's
Poems

What Mel Has Meant to Me

Mel had been the greatest husband
   A wife could ever want
He has been my eyes, my ears, my righthand man
   Always ready to help me out
So many times he has taken the time
   To tell me about the things I couldn't see
   The rabbits, squirrels, and birds
He took the time to explain the shows on tv
   Because I couldn't hear

   He took the time to explain to me
      What people were talking about
   For almost twenty-five years
      He has been everything to me
   He was a one-in-a-million kind of guy
      The one so precious to my heart
   I'll often be looking over my shoulder
      Expecting him to be there
   But he is in heaven now
      And I'm going to miss him very, very much

July 23, 1991

Verses to Dismissal Song

Let us rejoice
This is the day of the Lord
How generous is our Lord?
He gives to us without reservation

He gives us friends and family
to share our loves and sorrows
He who knows all
Gives us hope for our tomorrows!

For our Lord is all merciful
By helping others, we do the Lord's work
Administering to the sick
Helping others through grief
Just listening, caring and sharing!

The Lord is my Shepherd
How often have I knelt
And asked Him for help
And He softly touched my arm
And told me that He cared
I have felt the Lord
And I know He is there
In you and me

The Ushers

The ushers of Saints Charles and Helena
Look so grand in their attire
Dark pants, black tie and maroon jacket
So stately and distinguished

But I can tell you truthfully
That's just the surface
The ushers are the best of friends
Their hearts are made of gold

Their kindnesses are unsurpassed by human nature
The ushers are ready to lend a helping hand
They'll greet you with a smile
And the warmest handshake ever

They are men of God, we can be very proud
The finest ushers anywhere are our very own
Today we send a prayer to Him above
To bless them one and all

My Mom and Dad

The greatest gifts that ever lived

Are a Mom and Dad who care!

They give such tender love -

The love that we all crave

And need so very much!

I know because I have

Such a Mom and Dad

Two very special people

Beyond compare -

The greatest of the great

The best anywhere!

God has blessed me

    With so very much!

But I think the greatest gift

    He gave to me

Was my very own Mom and Dad

Their love for me shines through -

    The kindness, the joys, the tears

That we have shared from the cradle on

    And I love them so tenderly

Because they are my very own Mom and Dad

This and That

My writing hand is itching to get going
        But my mind just can't think today
So this will be a little verse of this and that
        There are so many things I'd like to say

Like Spring is lurking just around the corner
        Warm balmy days will soon be here
The birds will once again be singing their songs
        Of joy and love, always wonderful to hear

Loving, caring and sharing are precious expressions
        Of how we feel about our fellow man
These things no money on earth could ever buy
        Like a smile, they come from the inner heart

I'd like to speak of Mel and how I miss him so
        And about the joy and love of being a Grandma
Oh yes, I have two precious little grandsons
        A joy to Grandma's eye is Joshua and Brandon

This is just a little verse of this and that
        Of the things that come to mind today
Of all those precious, unforgettable moments
        That friends and family bring my way

February 24, 1995

A Honey of a Hairdresser

There is someone special in Clio

Whom I thought of from Kalamazoo

Cuz she does my hair so very nice

And it's always at a decent price

Sue perms it just the way I like

To me that's a number one STRIKE

She's a real honey of a hairdresser

And never would I ever trade her

I owe Sue the beauty credit always

Cuz my hair looks so nice nowadays

I know Sue is a 1981 Clio High grad

And it's the first year for her lad

Sue enjoys the verse and poetry I do

And I'm sure she'll love me so true

For writing her the neat little poem

And sending it from here to her home

This ode is bringing her a little fun

Sunny smiles and honest appreciation

March 3, 1998

Aaron and Stella

T'was sixty-three years ago

    On a rainy, warm Spring day

A young couple was in love ---

    He just eighteen, she sixteen

He was tall and handsome with red hair

    And his gray eyes, how they twinkled

She, too, was tall with auburn hair

    Her brown eyes smiling merrily

Their names, Aaron and Stella

    And it was their wedding day

After honeymooning in Battle Creek

    They set up housekeeping

And seven children did they raise ---

    Richard, William and Alberta

Karron, Mikeal, Patricia and Jack

    They worked very hard

And through good times and bad

    Their love and caring

Kept them going on and on ---

    Each passing year more precious than the last

Today, twenty grandchildren

>And twenty-nine great grandchildren later

Not to forget the great-great grandchildren, too

>Six decades and more have passed

Since the day they said "I do"

>Their hair has turned gray

And the aches and pains are there

>But their eyes still twinkle

(Though they're a little dimmer)

>The love and caring are still there

And all the fun besides

God has been very good to them

>He has blessed them many times over

My prayer for them today

>Is for many, many more precious memories

To hold within their hearts

Bob Stuart

Bob and Mel were two ushers

    At Saints Charles and Helena

They went to all the meetings

    And seemed to think alike

On what the Ushers' Club should do

    To help our parish out, so true

The volunteers you could count on

    No matter what the task may be

I never really met Bob Stuart

    Until my dear Mel passed on

I'm sure God whispered in his ear

    "Help this family, will you please?"

And like the good Christian he is

    He stepped out of the blue

Offering help in any way he could

    From legal matters and otherwise

Through it all, he stayed by our side

    Keeping us from washing away with the tide

There's no doubt within our hearts

    That's the Lord shining through

The kindness in his face

    The twinkle in his eyes

The love in his heart

    All these, and so much more

Not a penny would he take

    He found the time to give and give

The sacrifices he made for our family

    We'll not forget too soon

Yes, Bob and Mel were ushers

    Two very special people

And as I conclude this verse

    The tears are flowing once again

Mel is sadly missed by his family

    But I can smile through my tears

Mel is free from pain at last

    Bob is here to carry on as our friend

May God bless him and his family

    For a long, happy lifetime through

In appreciation

Jim and Carol

A warm, beautiful autumn

    The leaves, a spectacular sight to see

The perfect kind of fall

    When lovers are likely to meet

God looked down and decided

    Two hearts would meet at a football game

They were so young and free of heart

    Their eyes only meant for each other

Jim and Carol, by name

    Two future teachers, all the same

The wedding arrangements, and all

    Were set for June 8th at eleven

At St. James, a beautiful old church

    With marble floors and gold leafed paintings

The pastor, with a mind all his own

 Started down the aisle dressed in red

Instead of the traditional white

 Carol, beautiful in wedding gown

Walked down the aisle to Jim

 On the arm of her Uncle John

The Nuptial Mass had been written

 In little books for the guests

But the priest with a mind of his own

 Omitted the Nuptial Mass entirely

And said the Vigil Mass for the date

 They got to say their "I do's"

And that's the important part

 For God was there that day

And His blessings sent them on their way

 Amid a shower of rice upon leaving the church

At the reception, none other than Uncle John

    Presented Carol with her very first mop

To get her on the road to cleaning house

    After honeymooning in New York

They set up housekeeping in Lansing

    Where Jim was a student at MSU

God sent them three beautiful children

    Mark, Julie and Laura

Clio has been their home for fifteen years

    They've taught at Powers High for over twenty

God has walked with them

    Side by side for twenty-five years

He has blessed them on their way

    Through good times and bad

May His blessings and strength

    Continue on through the Golden Years

The Choir

The choir of Saints Charles and Helena

    Sing praises to our Lord

Their music rings throughout the church

    Bringing gladness sung from His Word

The choir, or are they angels?

    To me they look so pure

It wouldn't surprise me

    If they could fly away far

Our choir, the beautiful songs ring forth

    The wondrous praises to our Saviour

Oh, can't you just feel Him there

    Singing right along with us and our choir?

March 14, 1997

15

Father Paul Schwermer

Our parish was in despair
    Father Stockwell was retiring . . .
The search was on for a replacement
    Not just anyone would do
It must be a special priest
    Someone the parish could relate to
Father Paul came on the scene
    A whirlwind of youth and energy
All our prayers had been answered
    God sent His very best our way

He is a very special priest, indeed
    He'll sit amongst the little children
Telling stories, asking questions
    He blesses those too young for Communion
When the ushers get together
    You'll find him in their midst
Whenever there's work to be done
    Father Paul can be counted on
Our parish is quite fortunate
    He attacks everything with gusto

Now I wonder, where's the idea from
    To build Father Paul a patio
While he's off studying at St. Patrick's
    Way out west in California?

Noreen, today, gave me a hint
    Said she wanted to cover his "ugly" face
But I only see through my poet's eye
    And I could never, never tell a lie
The dream was Father Paul's
    The "welcome home" surprise is Father Jerry's

Now, Father Paul is human too
    He likes a good time and lots of fun
Enjoys fishing at a lake up north
    Loves to golf, there's that hole-in-one
The roller coaster rides at Cedar Point
    Are the ones you'll find him on
Father Paul likes to entertain his guests
    With a cold beer on the patio
But oh, he'd like some privacy
    To entertain his guests in peace

And all they had to do was ask

    For everyone loves Father Paul

The funds were very easy to raise

    Because he's liked so much by one and all

Now Father Paul can have his privacy

    And entertain his guests in peace

And we can thank our lucky stars

    God saw fit to send us Father Paul

May he be here at Saints Charles and Helena

    For many, many years to come

Merry Christmas

Christmas is not found in a big box
Beneath the Christmas tree
Christmas is found in the hearts
Of ordinary folks like you and me

The first Christmas happened long, long ago
When a Babe in swaddling clothes was born
The angels sang, the wise men came
The star led to Bethlehem that Christmas morn

Christmas, the celebration of Christ's birth
Should be spread in abundance through the year
In loving, caring and sharing toward our fellow man
Bringing JOY, HOPE, KINDNESS and CHEER

HAPPY BIRTHDAY, DEAR JESUS
Happy Birthday to You

Wishing all our friends and family
A BLESSED HOLIDAY SEASON
And GOOD HEALTH through the year

Love, Patty and Brian Grindel
Christmas 1996

Father Jerry

Father Paul has a very special friend
    Someone he met in his college days
Of course, everything he knows
    He learned from Father Jerry
Or was it the other way around?
    Did Father Jerry learn from Father Paul?
Whichever, it's open to discussion
    I kinda think they lean on each other
When Father Paul went off to St. Patrick's
    Father Jerry stepped right in

Father Jerry is a real wonder
    A really sensitive, understanding guy
I, myself, was deeply touched
    When he put out his hand to comfort my pain
He has done a great job right down to
    "The absence of Pious Piffle from the Pastor"
He celebrated his birthday with us
    And his eighteenth anniversary as a priest
Indeed, we have been truly blessed
    To have Father Jerry in our midst

What does Father Jerry like to do

    When he has time to call his own?

You might find him working in the soil

    Coaxing God's beautiful flowers to bloom

He enjoys music, and maybe a little dance

    And of course, he'll try the patio

Oh yes, his hair is turning gray

    And Noreen claims she gave him half

Father Jerry is, indeed, quite a gem

    And he has secured a place within our hearts

We're all going to miss him

    And we hope he'll stop back quite often

Evaluation at Jenkins

What'll I do but just sit here

 And wither to whiling my time?

Instead, I'll take pen in hand

 And a verse try to compose

I am so happy and full of energy today

 Just to be alive means a great deal

And to know He is here with me

Everyone seems so busy today

 But I wonder just what they'd think I do

If they knew how bored I am

 Sitting here whiling my time away?

A whole hour has come and gone

 And I'm still waiting patiently

But I know they'll soon be here

 And I'll be as busy as a humming bee

Oh, the evaluation week at Jenkins

    Goes flying by so very fast

Most of the tests I've liked thus far

    Except the crazy pattern puzzles

Some were quite easily figured

    But others drove the brain afrazzle

Not to forget the longest spelling test

    Forty-five words in three hours

The folks at Jenkins are very nice

    And I am glad to be here

My sense of humor can get in my way

    Most folks when I explain, understand

I did want to get on with the testing

    But lo and behold, the test was timed

So, I'll just patiently sit here waiting

My turn will soon be coming

Michigan Center for the Blind

In lovely Kalamazoo, there's a center for the blind

    Originally a hospital, it was constructed in 1969

You're made to feel real welcome and right at home

    When you first walk in the door, and then some

If you are hungry and haven't eaten, let them know

    They're there because they care and want to know

An experience you'll cherish a lifetime has begun

    The bond of friendship will be helpful anytime

You'll meet new friends in those hallowed halls

    In the cafeteria and all along those walls

It's really great to go up and down the halls

    Calling new friends by name and hearing your own

A sense of humor will go far and you'll laugh

    If someone can't see and sits in your lap

Maybe they'll bump into you from lack of sight

    And you'll both laugh and know it's all right

The unforgettable joking and bantering among the staff

 Could be the best therapy you can get for a laugh

"Baldy Jim" has names he figures suits his friends

 The woodcraft teacher, "Bald John", has a bare head

He claims someone took some shears and cut his hair

 Now I wonder did "Baldy Jim" do it for a fun flair?

He told me he cuts his friends hair for just $3.00

 But he'll be happy to do mine for free, no thanks

His friend, "Old Bob", a wonderful walking teacher

 Just two months makes him the oldest at the center

It seems to me that "Baldy Jim" pops up every time

 We go outside and it makes me laugh all the time

Because he tries hard to get me to call his friend

 A nice guy, "Old Bob" and there's never an end

And there's "Happy Judy" and "Thin Mary" too

 And I'll bet there are others knowing Jim as I do

I'm not quite sure how to conclude this verse

But I'm going to leave with a feeling of loss

This is a wonderful, joyful place beyond compare

It's unbelievable with all the fun and laughter

I love everyone, teachers, nurses, and janitors

The kitchen help, volunteers, and counselors

And the wonderful new friends I made along the way

They have a place in my heart, for them I pray

Happy Birthday, Jesus

Christmas Cheer, Christmas Joy

Found in the birth of a Baby Boy

So simple and humble was He

Born in a stable, son of Mary

Yet so pure, God's only Son

The animals so still, in adoration

This Babe was named Jesus

Who brought love and kindness

With His simple, humble birth

To spread everywhere over the earth

May your Christmas be humble

Like the simple, holy birth long ago

And may the brand new year

Bring peace and joy to all, far and near

Christmas 1997

Love, Patty and Brian

All About Me

This is a little verse about me, myself and I

    You see, these three happen to make up me

I've loved to read from the very beginning

    Westerns, history, comics and a good mystery

From the wee years, when I was just so tall

    You could find me in the forbidden haymow

I have always been stubborn and independent

    But never quite figured out how to milk a cow

Born Patricia Mae Karner August 28th in 1947

    A terrible fever made me very sick at five

And I had to repeat kindergarten over again

    But I've always felt happy just to be alive

Oh Lord, there are these little quirks of mine

    I'm very good at driving people up the wall

My tipsy, turvy balance gives me a terrible fear

    Because I never know when I am going to fall

I hear sneezes travel at a hundred miles an hour

    That's probably why they knock me off my feet

My eyes are deceiving and my ears follow suit

    But my heart's all right, that's what's sweet

T'was a drizzly, rainy day, September 3rd, 1966

    When Malcolm Grindel and I were united as one

The Lord granted us twenty-five beautiful years

    And three blessings; Melinda, Tammy and Brian

I'm mostly self-taught, I couldn't hear well

    I like to dance, play cards and have some fun

Also writing poetry is a pastime I really enjoy

    But Scrabble, Canasta and Euchre are still one

I don't quite know how to conclude this verse

    But I believe in the miracle of each new day

And know that I have much to be thankful for

    For the loving friends and family sent my way

Just Cuz the Money Is There

I took a walk along North Mill Street in Clio

    The beautiful old trees, so lovely for eyes to see

Through the years, they've spread their majestic limbs

    To give shade to everyone, including you and me

God planted those trees for us all to enjoy

    And many a bird has made a home there

But "progress" seems to be "in" these days

    The trees will come down cuz the money is there

Our City Fathers say the road has to be widened

    And, of course, the trees are in the way

They've stood there in majesty for a century, or so

    But "progress", it seems, is here to stay

I have lived in Clio my whole life through

    And I've seen progress in motion many a time

But one thing I hate with all my heart and soul

    Is to see the trees go, memories of a lifetime

I'm sure our City Fathers will have other excuses

    Like it should make the traffic go faster

But I, and many others, like Mill Street the way it is

    To many of us, it'll be "just cuz the money is there"

Dan and Debbie Markley

The golden sun is setting in the western sky

    The soft breeze blowing through my window

Whispering dainty little secrets in my ear

    About Dan and Debbie, folks I'd love to know

Debbie was a waitress at a bowling alley lounge

    And filling Dan with snacks became her passion

Love of bowling brought their hearts together

    Darts and horseshoes, too, got their attention

The judge gave out sentences, then cleared the room

    Dan Markley wed Debbie Johnson June 26, 1970

Now twenty-five years have come and gone, you know

    And June 17th, they'll renew their vows in church

God has blessed Dan and Debbie many times over

    Three lovely daughters Dawn, Michelle and Dana

All married now, and five sweet grandchildren

    Lauralyn, Samantha, Amber, April and Donny

In sickness and health, in work and play

    Dan and Debbie have shared many a good time

Their many friends and family join together today

    To wish the best as the wedding bells chime

Congratulations and best wishes

Dan Guzoziol (pronounced goose-joe)

These winter days are long, and oh, so cold

It warms the heart to think about good friends

There's a very special young man from Detroit

I met in Kalamazoo, in the summer of '93

He's the one the teachers always talked about

"Have you met Dan yet?" they would ask

"He's the one with a Cochlear implant

Maybe an implant could help you hear"

Daniel Thomas Guzoziol was born September 3, 1970

The fourth child of Faustine and Elaine Guzoziol

A miracle, he has survived a whole lot...

His left lung collapsed not once, but twice

He lost his hearing, and his eyes got bad

In March of '79, he was diagnosed with leukemia

June 6, 1981 was a special occasion for Dan

His sister, Nancy, gave him the "gift of life" that day

Dan grew up around the Detroit area

    Enjoying life with his brothers and sisters

Attending St. Bart's and St. Florian Catholic Schools

    His outlook on life is excellent, his desire strong

I have never heard him complain, not ever

    (He gives his mother due credit for that)

Dan has a wonderful sense of humor. (That helps)

    He admits with laughter when he makes a mistake

    Since Dan is deaf he knows sign language

        His hands often moving too fast for me

    At the Blind Center, he'd sit by the window

        The best place to watch the action go by

    Dan and I are both avid Detroit Tiger fans

        And he kept me up to date on the baseball games

    Dan's ambition is to be a computer programmer

        And by God's Grace, he's going to make it

My Friend Sandy

Sandy and I were in Mr. Tom Gross' English class

Both of us Juniors back in September of 1964

Sandy talked slowly and her arms moved along, too

A kinship turned friendship over thirty years ago

Because of her arms, she couldn't write like us

And depended on Mom for getting the homework done

Sandy fought and broke the barriers, paving the way

For the handicapped to attend regular classrooms

Sandra Jane Newberry was born on Good Friday in 1947

As the elder daughter of Floyd and Joyce Newberry

Sandy was born back first during Flint's Great Flood

With limited muscle use, a victim of cerebral palsy

Not expected to live more than a few short months

    Sandy is a perfect example that miracles do happen

Her family just didn't accept what the doctors said

    She reads the Bible daily, a born again Christian

Sandy is very special, she's smart and a great friend

    And when helping her mom by doing the dinner dishes

No kidding, everything else ends up spotlessly clean

    The curtains, the windows, the floor and the dishes

I don't get to see Sandy as often as I'd like these days

    But we don't give up, we depend on the regular mail

For Sandy can type, never fear, and type along she does

    Through the years her letters have come without fail

Wishing you the best, Sandy

To the Army Reunion - September 1995

What a wonderful thrill to be on the go once again
   From our own unique state of Michigan
On through Ohio, just a little of Pennsylvania
   And following the mountains through West Virginia

The beautiful mountains, so hazy in the distance
   Reaching up and up and seeming to touch the sky
And every rig I see, makes me think of a special guy
   As we go coasting along the Maryland highway

In West Virginia, we stopped by the wayside
   For a picnic of crackers, bologna and melon
The hot wind blowing so very, very hard
   Made me wonder about "Hurricane Marilyn"

Way back during World War II, in the 1940's
   Companies A, B and C and rescue headquarters
Made up the 609th Destroyer Battalion
   With Sgt. Frank Karner in charge of one tank

Each year, the third weekend in September is set aside
    With much ado and fanfare for the army reunion
Of the gallant men and women who fought
    Without reservations to keep our country free

Good-byes were said on a rainy Sunday afternoon
    And we started the nine hundred mile journey home
The reds and golds mixed in with the greens
    Were a sure sign that fall had come to the mountains

Back through Virginia, Maryland and West Virginia
    And a picnic with the wasps flying everywhere
Keeping us on our toes, dodging their stings
    We're looking forward to what next year brings

Karen

I find my heart so heavy today

A beautiful person has left us so sudden

"Beautiful inside, as well as outside"

A description she gave to someone else

Never realizing she was describing herself

I'm sure she'd be honored to know

She's thought of in this special way

By those of us who love her so

Karen lived her life to the fullest

With never a word of complaint

She always seemed to be doing her part

Thinking of how she could help the other fella

She carried the Karner trait of a happy smile

That brightened the room as she entered

Her belief in God was her strength

Her example she has passed on to us

Karen Karner married Leonard Walther, Jr.

On a snow stormy weekend in April of '75

She turned out to be a real homemaker

The best there ever could be

Her meals were made from scratch

She'd always be trying a new recipe

But her recipe for being Karen shines through

The many gestures of love she left for us all

I have never liked saying good-byes

And the final ones are the hardest of all

It's so hard to believe she's gone

In our hearts, we will remember Karen

For the kind, loving person she was

But knowing Karen is in Heaven

Waiting for each of us with outstretched arms

Should help ease the grief just a little

In loving memory

Ed

I seem to write my best at night
  When thoughts of those I love keep me awake
So here I am at midnight
  And my thoughts have turned to Ed
He has no idea, I am sure
  Just how many nights he keeps me up
For my nerves have never rested
  Since the day I met that guy

Ed is always hard at work
  With little time to call his own
And though he'd rather go fishing
  He seems inclined to keep on working
You can find him almost anywhere
  Between Michigan, Ohio, and West Virginia
He's always on the go, that guy
  His watch, his constant companion

Ed only has a fifth grade education
    But of course, he's super smart
He is a jack-of-all-trades
    There's nothing he can't do
No job is too big or too small
    From building houses to putting up clotheslines
From building roads to just being Ed
    He has a special place within our hearts

This wonderful guy never struts his feathers
    He's one of the guys in a pair of jeans
He's a real down-to-earth guy I know
    Drives around in a '79 Ford
We know our time with him is precious
    He'll soon be on the go again
And once again, we'll all be asking
    "Have you seen or heard from Ed?"

Whatever you do, wherever you go, take care
You are a one-in-a-million kind of guy

My Parish Family

We have learned to be a loving parish family

Since our beginning nearly forty years ago

From the time of our beginnings

On down through the years

We have felt God's everlasting Love and Presence

He has softly touched our hearts

And led us through good times and stormy seas

From Father Horton to Father Paul Groan

We're always getting compliments from visitors

"The parishioners here are very friendly"

We're the best by far in all the land

God's love is here for all to see

We know it's the little things that matter

Like enfolding one in a great big hug

Or just a smile, and a kind word, too

That's the Lord shining through us all

We have grown through God's love

From just a church, then a rectory

Now, we have the C. Robert Stockwell Center

And, of course, our September Festival

Which is loads and loads of fun

And brings us all together as one

The fun, laughter and tears that we have shared

Has brought out the best in all of us

I have been blessed with many friends

There are so many, I can't count

And each and everyone has touched my heart

Each one of you, a gift from God

When I was in my darkest hours

You have never let me down

I have felt the Lord so very much

Shining through you, my Parish Family

God bless you all

Maureen Anderson

How little I knew Maureen, yet how much

We met in the middle of June, in Kalamazoo

I had no roommate for two weeks, and more

When running in from the lounge, there she was

She was tall, 5'10", with curly, red hair

And had no trouble hiding behind Evan

For he was even taller than she, at over six feet

We hit it off from the start, she and I

Maureen was blind, couldn't tell night from day

But accepted it with a grace that was all her own

We would sit and talk for hours and hours on end

It helped that she could talk with the moving hand

I seem to have a knack for driving people crazy

And Maureen was no exception to the rule

When I didn't respond to something she'd said

She'd stare at me, "Patty, are you listening?"

Maureen had a wonderful sense of humor

Just the sight of her would get me laughing

And we seemed to agree on one important point

That it's better to laugh than to cry

Our phone conversations were full of laughter

One night when I called, she spilled her popcorn

With glee, I said I'd be right out and help clean up

She responded, "Yes, please, and hurry up"

My friend, Maureen, was very sick and in a lot of pain

She'd said she was getting better, slowly but surely

But God took her Home on a cold Sunday afternoon

She just slipped quietly away into Eternity.

I'll always have beautiful memories of her

The times when I was down, and she lifted me up

Her encouragement meant a great deal to me

She always said, "Life goes on," and so it does

In loving memory

Gertie Vuillemot

Right in the middle of a big snowstorm

The snow so beautiful, drifting higher

What better way to spend a winter afternoon

Than to write about a sweetheart named Gertie

She is one of my favorite, all around fans

Every verse I write, she has to have a copy

Gertrude Coates was born on Independence Day, 1926

That happened to be our nation's 150th birthday

It was a beautiful, sunny May Day, 1945

When Gertrude Coates married Louis Vuillemot

Word War II was not quite over

When they were united in Holy Matrimony

They set up housekeeping and started a family

God sent seven beautiful children their way

Judy, James, John, and Robert

Mark, Karen and Mathew

Twenty-eight years of married bliss they had

Before Louis left for his Heavenly Home

A mother with young children, she couldn't drive

Life became a real struggle for Gertie

Today, Gertie is a proud grandmother

God has tested her faith many times over

Through it all, she has emerged with flying colors

She takes life with a grain of salt and a sense of humor

There are many things Gertie likes to do

When she gets in the mood for having fun

Like word search puzzles, and euchre games

And seeing what's on sale at rummage sales

When I was wheelchair bound, and in a bad mood

She'd take me on a real joy ride, what fun it was

Around and around the store we would go

She at the controls, me screaming, "Slow down"

God bless you, Gertie

God's Promise

Do you know the story behind the rainbow?
    It's a special promise God made to mankind
When pointed out to me, I can see the rainbow
    Making its beautiful way across the skyline

Thousands and thousands of years ago
    God looked down with a heavy heart on His people
And witnessed the wickedness and greed
    And only one family lived according to His Will

Of all the people here on God's beautiful earth
    Noah and his family lived by God's Word
God spoke to Noah and told him of His plans
    Telling him to warn the people of the coming flood

But people are people, and wouldn't believe
  So Noah and his sons worked on the ark
While people went on with their wicked ways
  And soon found the warning was right on the mark

God lined up all the animals, two by two
  And with Noah's family were safe in the ark
Then God sent the rain, forty days and nights
  Finally, the people understood, but too late

Noah and his family had to wait patiently
  Until the dove returned with a green leaf
And God put His beautiful rainbow in the sky
  As His promise never again to cause such grief

Today, when you see a softly colored rainbow
  Stretching across the sky after a big downpour
Remember the promise God made long, long ago
  And you'll know God never lets us down

Friends

There are so many friends
I've made in Kalamazoo
And I'll never forget them
When I am home again in Clio!

They are very special friends
That have touched me
In one way or another
And very grateful, I'll ever bet

They may have just said
"Good morning, Patty"
But those are music to my ears
And it means so much to me!

Kindnesses can't be forgotten
And they're treasures in my heart.
Hertha works in the nurse's office
And was ever so kind from the start

She pried through my computer
And found my lost document
Hertha is wonderful in many ways
I'm happy to make this testament

Peggy is also a blessing here
And told me about the drummers
I really enjoyed their sweet music
So nice for all students and teachers!

Newt, Deb, Robin, Mary and two Kims
Are all friends I made in Kalamazoo
But there are many, many more
I'll remember from my home in Clio!

This is my last day at the center
And every kindness is a treasure
These friends I've made, new and old
Have brought me such pleasure!

Special People

It takes a very special kind of person

To want to help others any way they can

I returned to Kalamazoo to learn computer

And I admit, I wouldn't mind coming again!

Some of the most wonderful people work here

At the Michigan Training Center for the Blind

They have such beautiful hearts of patience

And I feel very privileged to know their kind!

Wendy was my teacher for first hour typing class

And said there was only one way to learn computer

Touch-typing was very difficult in the beginning

But I'm happy I stuck it out for I'm no quitter!

Then there was Barb, my individual instructor

Who taught me about the keyboard ups and downs

She instructed how to save on the floppy disk

Typeover, printing and centering of my poems

Ken and Rosnani were my walking companions

To the store, in town and through the parks

We'd stop to enjoy nature and flower blossoms

And continue on our way when the dog barks.

Roger is the one looked up to for answers

To the most complicated computer questions

He has been doing computers for ten years

And knows sign that helps in situations!

I can't forget the afternoon teachers

Who did their best to pass the time away

Crafts, woodwork, sign language, cooking

Karen said creativity is better any day!

"Baby Jim" Baird now teaches woodcrafts

And knows a lot about mending things

Jim turned fifty on March eighteenth

He's well known for his humor flings

Mary taught me some sign I didn't know

And I taught Lynne some hand language

Most craft classes were full of crafters

And their products will get much usage

That covers my regular teachers nicely

Now I will have to write another verse

The substitutes are also a special brand

And I'd like to remember them in prose!

Inner Peace

Writing is therapy for the soul
    It has to come out, that I am afraid
I put my heart in Jesus' loving hands
    And my aches and doubts drain away

    I put my trust and faith in Jesus
        He knows without a doubt what's best
    On my knees, I ask for His forgiveness
        And pray that He will give my heart rest

Oh Jesus, my soul to Thee, I give
    Take me now, and give me Your peace
Ease my burdens, stay with me til eternity
    As I pour out my innermost heart to Thee

    Jesus, I know You are forever near at hand
    All I need do is ask for Your Guidance
And follow in Your Way, Your Truth
    Take my soul, Dear Jesus, it is Yours

    Jesus, His tenderness and love are mine
    And I feel my burdens swept away
    His Inner Peace has come into my heart
    And I thank Him for being there for me

November 1, 1995

THANKSGIVING

Turkey, dressing, and all the fixins

Harvest sharing and family mixins

An age old tradition going back to Pilgrim times

New lands and new frontiers had to be won

Kings and dictators had to be fought

Suffering and strife had to be conquered

Giving thanks to God for seeing them through

Indians helping enhance the festive mood

Visions of freedom they'd never known before

Invisible, yet felt, the Guiding Hand of the Lord

Now, today, we still gather around our tables

Giving thanks to God for His Love and easing our troubles

Happy Thanksgiving to all

Michigan Weather

Michigan weather is full of surprises
    From day to day, and week to week
We never can tell what the weather will be
    It may snow in June, or rain in January

Michigan weather is full of surprises
    This winter is a beautiful example, by far
It's spring one week, and winter the next
    We're wondering if Mother Nature is all mixed up

Michigan weather is full of surprises
    'Tis January, and joggers are running in shorts
Oh, what will the groundhog think
    When he comes out to check for spring?

Michigan weather is full of surprises
    The climate here is always changing...
It's wonderful to have spring in winter
    And from me, there'll be no complaining

January 16, 1995

Winter's Last Hurrah

I looked outside my window this morning
 And the earth was all covered with snow
It seemed more like January than March
 The diamonds out there aren't to stay, I know

It's cold, it's freezing, yet so beautiful
 Because it's really winter's last hurrah
Lots of children will bundle up warm as toast
 And go sledding down the Pine Run Hill

March winds will soon blow winter's wrath away
 Mother Earth will once again turn green
The grass will grow and the birds will sing
 Also, the Pine Run Creek will flow free

Yearly, winter and spring have to fight it out
 It's as natural as counting one, two, three
It's so hard to feel "down in the dumps"
 Cuz I have "spring fever" and it will be

We have to make the best and enjoy the illusions
 So bundle up snug and warm with childish glee
And go sledding, sliding, or build a snow fort
 Last, but not least, enjoy winter's last hurrah

March 5, 1996

Autumn

I took a little walk along the bike path today
    The sun so warm upon my cheek
Made it hard to believe summer has come and gone
    And autumn begins this week

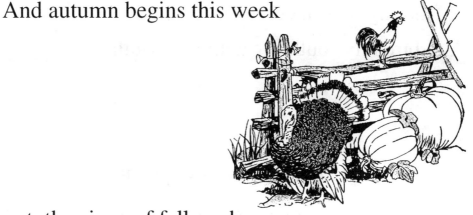

But yet, the signs of fall are here
    The days are getting shorter
And the nights are getting longer
    There's a coolness in the twilight air
That wasn't there before

The school bells are once more ringing
    And the kids are back to basics
There's football games and apple fests
    And harvest times and homemade pumpkin pies

Mother Nature is getting all dressed up
   In all her breathtaking glory
Oh, those leaves we'll have to rake
   Hunting season comes in autumn
And birds fly south for winter warmth

   Halloween will soon be here
      Witches and goblins roaming our streets
'Tis followed closely by Thanksgiving
      When we share the fruits of our labors
   And give thanks for all those we hold dear

I wish all my new neighbors at Pine Creek Manor
   A happy fall

Kimberly Keidel

This is the same place I met the other Kim

Who lived in the apartment across the hall

Kim Keidel is a very impressive, young woman

Who has learned to care, love and stand tall!

Kimberly Marie Keidel born September 14, 1964

Is the oldest of Jerry and Nancy's six children

The others are two brothers and three sisters

In order, Kevin, Kris, Laura, Kelly and Steven

Kim's childhood was near Michigan's west coast

Between Ludington and Grand Haven, in Muskegon

The love of Kim's life is a mixed cocker-mutt

She's fifteen years old and named Cinnamon

Cinnamon and Kim's lives are very much alike

Because they've been victims of other's rages

They've survived alcoholism, drugs and abuses

And it has taken a lot of faith and courage!

Kim has been diabetic for eleven years now

And coping has been a tremendous struggle

The doctor predicted she'd be blind shortly

But this didn't happen and it's a miracle!

Kim has worked as a licensed practical nurse

And loves working in nursing and group homes

She likes working in crafts and helping others

And really seems to enjoy reading my poems!

Happiness and love are found within ourselves

And it's something special Kim has to share

She has set a goal to make her life much better

If Kim can, others can, for to love is to care!

I have enjoyed talking to Kim through the relay

And can't end this without referring to Keidel

You see, Kim's a sign language student of mine

Also, her last name rhymes nicely with Grindel!

Florida Bound and Back

Michigan had ice here, there and everywhere
    And I longed for warm days and sunny skies
A week in Florida seemed the perfect remedy
    A time of nostalgia with my friend, Phyllis

I hadn't seen Phyllis in nearly ten years
    But the years were soon wiped away
And it seemed more like just yesterday
    As we settled down to a good Scrabble game

Brian and I roamed all over St. Petersburg
    Took lots of pictures and got some sunburn
We toured an art museum with Phyllis
    And saw an interesting Russian exhibit

Busch Gardens is a beautiful place to see
    Giant turtles, alligators and all the greenery
And jumping hungrily for food in the water
    Were the biggest goldfish I ever did see

We went on a picnic at a nature resort
    The weather was perfect, sunny, windy and warm
And big bubbles coming up from the creek
    Indicated an alligator, or more, just might be there

We're back home in Michigan once more
    The ice is melted, trees are budding
Florida is nice for spending the winters

March 27, 1995

My Time

My time is told by the writer's chime
    That keeps these words on the rhyme

It can happen any time, day or night
    My mind rules my soul with its might

Words are the magic possessing my soul
    Bringing forth their messages of truth

My thoughts can be the simplest of things
    When I write, I see what my pen brings

Father Time seems in the biggest hurry
    I can't understand his driving flurry

A writer's crime is in the lack of sleep
    Nothing stops my thinking, words to keep

So I have to try and make each day count
    Twenty-four hours is no large amount

The years go rolling onward through the ages
    I haven't figured any of the fleeing images

This is just a silly little harmless ditty
    But my time, the writer's crime is poetry

I love to write and my thoughts are here
    If you like to read, there's good there

March 12, 1997

Lady of the Manor

Cheerful, friendly, polite

    Always doing what's right

Spreading cheer and laughter

    With happiness trailing after

Patti Grindel is her name

    And Patti is always the same

She loves teddy bears, loves to talk

    She loves to go for daily walks

She plays cards and checkers, too

    Has a high I.Q., that's a match for you

by I. B. Me (Don Kaake) February 19, 1997

Don Kaake

April 1996, Jill and I were playing Yahtzee

When this frail man in a wheelchair

Came on a manor tour with Patti Kaake

Don Kaake's his name and he had cancer

Being here, making friends at the manor

Has helped Don on the road to recovery

His Clio stories are something to be told

If he'll write what he knows for me

Don's a Clio man, a good fellow through

Miss Boyse taught him three times in school

Imagine my surprise this rainy morning

When he gave me his poem of two days ago

He says he's no poet, tell me again anytime

After reading page 68, he does just fine

Sweet Irene

On a cold winter's day, I look outside my window

    And see diamonds sparkling in the fresh fallen snow

And 'tis my favorite time of year to take pen in hand

    And write about special people I've come to know

Way back in 1910, when cars were something new

    A young couple, Frank and Josephine Kiljanski

Proudly made plans for daughter, "Sweet Irene"

    Who arrived to enhance their world on October 4th

Irene grew up in the Flint area, a joy to all who knew her

    It was in the 1930's, during "The Great Depression"

She was working in a Secretary of State's office

    When William Nagle walked in to do his business

That's how they met, and the courtship began

    It was a beautiful, warm day of June 5th, 1937

When William and Irene were wed by Fr. Okk in St. Michael's

    Beginning a fifty year lifetime of love and happiness

There's no doubt within my mind, they worked very hard

    She in the Secretary of State's office, and a teacher, too

And he as a plant analyst at Buick, Oh times were hard

    And our country was on the brink of World War II

God sent this wonderful couple three beautiful children

    Their daughter, Pat, grew up to be a nurse

Daughter, Mary, grew up to be a teacher, like Mom

    And William, Jr., who followed Dad into Buick

Yes, indeed, there's a very special, sweet lady...

    Her faith in God is strong, and we love her a whole lot

Together, Willie and I take her Holy Communion

    And have a nice visit and a good chat twice each month

"Sweet Irene" loves little children and helps in school

    And all the children love her in return

For there's one, and only one "Sweet Irene"

    The one who shares and has a heart of pure gold

January 9, 1995

Frank and Irene

There's a special couple more dear to my heart
    Than any words could ever impart
And over the years, no matter what desires they had
    They've always found time to help and to guide
I have known these two from the cradle on
    Frank and Irene, or to me, Dad and Mom

Frank and Irene met at a dance in Gagetown
    In April 1940, she was seventeen and he twenty-four
World War II intervened and Frank went off to war
    Irene waited patiently, four long years, and more
Francis Michael Karner wed Irene Harriet Hitler
    At St. Agatha Church in 1945, the 20th of October

This beautiful couple I know so well
    Started life in Flint, then moved to Clio
They've both worked very hard over the years
    Farming, banking, clerking and working at GM
God sent them five beautiful children
    Shirley, Patricia, Janet, Larry and Karen

For many have been the storms along the way
　　And their greatest heartbreaks of all time
Were losing a "son," Mel, in the summer of '91
　　And God called Karen home just two years later
Though their hearts are broken, their love goes on
　　Sharing and caring and always being there for us all

Yes, Frank and Irene, a wonderful example to all
　　What beautiful, loving memories I can recall
They are seventeen grandchildren strong
　　And open their hearts to those in need
They have an unwavering faith and trust in God
　　We wish the best for the "Golden Years" and beyond

Ryan and Derek

What a beautiful morning we have today
    A lovely, sunny day in the middle of May
And my thoughts have turned to two little boys
    But 'tis 1995 and they are little no more

Ryan Edward, born on Leap Year Day in 1976
    And Derek Lee, born June 12th the following year
Are the two sons of Ronald and Karen Stanbaugh
    Two little boys I have known from day one

We lived side-by-side their growing up years
    And looking out our windows, we would see
Ryan and Derek out playing or riding their bikes
    Or joining Dad in a baseball game or horseshoes

Winters, they'd be out building a snowman
    Summers found them building camps in the woods
And I fondly recall two considerate little boys
    Helping their neighbors whenever they could

Ryan, like Dad, is a horseshoe pitching enthusiast
    And won the championship in the summer of '93
After school, Derek has been in the police cadets
    Holds rank of lieutenant and the Sheriff's Awards

Time has flown by, but where has it gone?
    Ryan and Derek are now handsome young men
Ryan might become a builder, Derek a policeman
    Whatever their choice, I wish them the very best

Congratulations on your graduation day

Linda Healan

More than thirty years have come and gone
    Since I first set eyes on Linda back in '64
Her sister, Sandy, was in my English class
    And I happened to meet Linda after school

Linda Marie Newberry was born June 28, 1948
    The second daughter of Floyd and Joyce Newberry
And she grew up here and there around Flint
    Living in Wind Drift Trailer Park when we met

Linda met Gerald Healan at Fenton Family Restaurant
    She as a waitress, and he her customer
Their love blossomed and they wed the first of June, 1968
    And three children did they have: Dawn, Brian and Tammy

Jerry and Linda bought a house in Montrose
    Things just didn't work out, and Jerry left
Leaving Linda to raise her three babies alone
    Times were hard, but Linda did her very best

We rarely saw them over the next few years
   But somehow time slipped away, as it does
The children grew up and Linda moved to Clio
   Helping others keeps Linda on her toes

Things and times are still hard for Linda
   As she's forever and ever looking for work
But it's the little things that bring enjoyment
   Like reading, crocheting and she likes to cook

I wish her the best of luck always

Ron Pung

It's the corny hours of a hot June night
    When sleep eludes me, and I need to write
My thoughts have gone back a few years
    To a little boy so brown from the sun
And I recall remarking to his mom
    Just how much Ronnie looked like Ron

Ronald James Pung, born Memorial Day, 1976
    Is the son of Ronald and Jacqueline Pung
Ronnie was less than two months old
    When Ron and Jackie adopted him on July 22nd
And Ronnie knows with all his heart and soul
    How very blessed he is for his loving parents

From the time Ronnie was a little toddler
    He's never considered walking around a mud puddle
It has always been right straight through
    And even today, it's the only way to go
Water sports top the list of Ronnie's favorites
    Water skiing and swimming in the lake up north

Ronnie has hated school from kindergarten on
　　Must be the lack of mud puddles in the classroom
Some little birdie whispered in my ear
　　That Ronnie won the mock award this year
For the boy most likely to be out of class
　　And has a knack for looking busy in the halls

Ron has grown into a handsome young man
　　And this year graduates from Powers Catholic High
It's time to set aside the excuses for avoiding class
　　And decide on a goal for the future
Whatever his choice, wherever he goes
　　May God be his guide and success his goal

Congratulations on your graduation day

Don and Verna Allett

Looking back, I still see Don sitting there
　Glasses off, squinting at the Bible's words
And I knew without a doubt, we'd be friends
　In class, that's how we met Don and Verna

Don and Verna are a very special twosome
　Who met at a St. Patrick's dance for singles
A whirlwind five month courtship they had
　Before being united as one at St. Leo's

Don Felix Allett married Verna May Dunn
　On a sunny, warm August 16th in 1975
Or did Don marry the microphone, I wonder
　For Verna claims he didn't look at her

Together Don and Verna built a good life
　Don's ambition was to become a chemist
But he's now on the road to a new career
　And Verna takes good care of elderly folks

Don and Verna enjoy walking in the park
    For he is whole with Verna by his side
Blindness has taken his sight, not his spirit
    He uses his cane and she is his guide

Verna enjoys singing in the church choir
    But Don claims he can't carry a tune
But he listens to the birds in the summer
    And can tell their species by their sound

They both have a wonderful sense of humor
    And their love and need for each other
Can go a long, long way when need arises
    Also, their faith in God holds together

May God as Blessings be theirs for many years

Father Paul Guoan

I was in Kalamazoo in the summer of '93
    When Bishop Povish's news came to me
Father Paul Schwermer would be leaving
    For a more tasking job at Holy Rosary

God sent us a soft spoken Father Paul Guoan
    And as he walked around the parish grounds
A satisfied little smile lit up his face
    He'd be happy at Chuck and Helen's Place

Father Paul has an abundance of love to give
    An inheritance from his big, loving family
Of seven brothers and sisters and parents too
    He told me himself, he's right in the middle

There's always something wonderful going on
    When Father Paul goes on his busy, busy way
He starts his day with morning Mass at 8:30
    And continues his good deeds through the day

To speak of many things, sometimes just a few
    Father Paul helps with Vincent de Paul
If someone's sick, he takes his job to heart
    And does whatever he can to lend a hand

Father Paul loves and adores little children
    Many a time, inviting them to the altar
When babies are baptized before Sunday Mass
    They join in the limelight in his arms

When he finds time, he works in the yard
    Singing a lovely song as he goes along
"Playing" his accordion, piano or organ
    For he has a flair for music and song

Father Paul is a very loving, caring person
    At K of C, he's a chaplain "Faithful Friar"
With a marvelous sense of humor and wit
    And we thank the Good Lord, he's all ours

March 15, 1996

Puzzles

There are so many different kinds of puzzles
    Jigsaw, crossword and search for a word
But some of the most fascinating kinds
    Are the ones my mind tries to absorb

Like why is that car just sitting over there?
    I know whose car it is, but I can't see
So when I get a chance, I call and ask why?
    It turns out they were just waving to me

Now, we're gathered in a meeting room
    The speaker has white hair and a white robe
And, oh Lord, the wall is also white as snow.
    I can hear him, but my eyes have to probe

My ears can't seem to figure the mystery
    Of a mumble from a growling grumble
There seems to be too many tongue twisters
    And it sure can make my mind stumble

Those people just standing there in the hall

    Who are they, friend or foe, what do they want?

I just have to get a lot closer to see who

    They aren't just shadows, they're my friends

I cannot figure out some hard core mysteries

    Of why people go around with a scowl and frown

When the day is beautiful and things are OK

    Why they drown in misery and let things go down

The world is full of different puzzles to solve

    Maybe as many as different people on earth

But one thing for sure, happiness is within

    And many things can be better with a smile

Just Ask Brian

Brian is my son, as you might know
    He's the guy with all the answers
From the time when he was just so small
    Everything had to be exactly correct

Mrs. Eastman was his kindergarten teacher
    And whenever she asked what time it was
His answer was always to the exact minute
    Never a bit of rounding off for him

Brian has been hearing impaired all his life
    And learned sign language at Tuuri Mott
So now, we have a sign language expert
    Woe to the person who makes a mistake

In spelling, he's the best you can find
    Many folks spell the way the word sounds
But not my Brian, it has to be correct
    And that goes for punctuation, too

If you are overweight or have a bad heart
    Be sure to ask Brian, "the health expert"
He will tell you to do one hundred push-ups
    And twenty times to lift those weights

On the roads, Brian goes the speed limit
    And curses all the drivers going over
He hates all tailgaters with a vengeance
    Because they can make him lose control

If it's money you need, just ask Brian
    His way is to rob a bank for a million
But Brian is as honest as anyone can be
    This is in jest, don't take it seriously

One thing that's for sure, you can't be bored
    The trick is to get him in conversation
About anything and everything, just ask Brian
    I know without a doubt, he'll have an answer

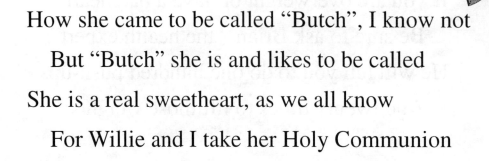

Butch

How she came to be called "Butch", I know not
　　But "Butch" she is and likes to be called
She is a real sweetheart, as we all know
　　For Willie and I take her Holy Communion

Born Margery Kleiber December 23rd in 1941
　　She grew up the baby of her loving family
Of four brothers and one sister, Carol
　　And somehow, the name "Butch" came to be

Butch is someone very, very extra special
　　For God made her that way as only He can
She folds her hands lovingly over her Rosary
　　And says "The Our Father" so solemnly

Butch is the proudest Godmother I've known
　　To Joel, her nephew's cute little boy
I've never heard a Godmother talk so often
　　About a Godson. He must be a real joy

Rosie is Butch's cute little white doggie

   And her bark is always worse than her bite

She takes no heed when told to "Get down"

   But Butch loves her with all of her might

Posters, shirts and a statue of "The King"

   Elvis Presley never had a more doting fan

Her bedroom is full of his memorabilia

   For Butch gets his souvenirs whenever she can

Butch is one of the sweetest folks we've known

   It's always a real pleasure to visit with her

And we know God has a very special place

   In His ever loving heart reserved for her

Libby

When I came to Kalamazoo, Libby was here
    Such a sweet girl, she's a real dear!
Libby doesn't seem to mind my deafness
    She has a lot of patience and kindness

Patience can come from a large family
    Her parents are Harold and Audrey Magee
She has seven brothers and four sisters
    And is the youngest of the daughters

Libby's Dad worked as a city truck driver
    And her mom sewed as a canvase stitcher
Northern Michigan was where they resided
    And their large, loving family was raised

Libby Jean Magee grew up near Traverse City
    And enjoys visiting her friends and family
She also likes to play pool, work on crafts
    Talk on the phone, eat and make little gifts

All bright colors are Libby's favorite colors,
    Blues, greens, reds, golds; lovely splendors
Her travels have been around Michigan, Indiana
    Also through Kentucky and south to Louisiana

I just noticed something special about Libby
    She's exactly eight years older than my baby
Brian, my son, and Libby are December babies
    And I'll be able to remember which is Libby's!

At one pound ten ounces, Libby was a miracle
    And in 1962, that must have been an obstacle
Libby Jean was born three months premature
    Because she was due in March, not December!

Well, it's fast approaching a brand new day
    And at this computer, I'd sure love to stay
Libby would like to keep in touch by Braille
    So I think I have a brand new Braille pen pal

An Open Letter to My Grandsons

Dear Joshua and Brandon,

Today is Memorial Day, 1996, and I can't sleep

There's a need within my heart to write

It's been nearly five years since my heart broke

And God took your grandpa from my side so quick

I have such wonderful memories of your grandpa

He was special, the guy I needed and loved most

Not a day went by that he didn't show me in all ways

Just how much he cared, and loved me the most

On a cold day thirty years ago, we went to the prom

He put his arms around me to keep me warm

Your grandpa wasn't much of a dancer back then

But I loved to dance and he learned with a charm

Grandpa and I were wed thirty years ago this year

    And your aunt Melinda came on June 7th, 1967

It was Wednesday and I'd been doing the laundry

    And didn't know I'd be a Mom that evening

Less than two years later, on Mother's Day

    Just seventeen minutes before midnight May 11th

Your mom entered the world, our smallest baby

    We had two lovely girls, Melinda and Tammy

But our little family was not yet complete

    God sent your uncle Brian the very next year

He was our biggest baby at seven pounds and more

    And arrived just twenty days before Christmas

Grandpa had arthritis from the age of sixteen

    But never let it hinder him in any way

He worked at General Motors for twenty-five years

And looked forward to retirement and play

Life isn't all roses, this we knew and accepted

Melinda was sick at eighteen months with fever

And Brian had pneumonia at the age of one

But our faith and trust in God never wavered

We enjoyed camping trips, biking, playing games

And your mommy and daddy were wed July 1st, 1988

Your grandpa's hair turned gray much too soon

And people asked him if I were his daughter

People tell me often that you look like Grandpa

And I know in my heart, he's happy up above

Proud as any loving Grandpa could ever be

To have two adorable little Grandsons to love

Lew and I

It's the wee hours of a freezing cold night
    And I just got to thinking about ice and snow
And I have a fear of falling on the icy way
    As I try to keep my balance with a good foothold

There's a very special guy just waiting for me
    And it seems like an eternity I've waited
He'll soon be free to stay by my side forever
    Of this I'm sure we're well mated

His only desire is to love me til eternity
    And to take care of me until the end of time
Our best years still lie ahead of us
    The kids are grown and we're still in our prime

So, a trucking we will go and have loads of fun
    I'll teach him canasta and also to sign
He will take me wherever I want to go; anywhere
    Together we'll go through life, side by side

We were meant for each other, Lewis and Patricia
    And never have I ever written so much, so close
As these three glorious days, I pour my heart
    On the paper, in my favorite prose

Jacob and Laura Hiller

Memories can be ever so sweet to recall, you see
    Especially when it's Grandpa and Grandma
And such fond memories I have of them in my heart
    Coming back into focus are Jake and Laura

Jacob Jesse Hiller, born September 3rd, 1887
    And Laura McConnell, born November 11th, 1894
Grew up in Michigan's thumb area near Cass City
    Met and were married the third of April, 1918

In January of 1919, a son Floyd Leslie was born
    And daughter, Irene Harriet, in December 1922
Jake was a farmer and did his plowing by horse
    And Laura was mother, the stay at home kind, too

Jake had bad eyes from his childhood forth
    And drove a car just once, right in the ditch
So then by choice, he left the driving to Laura
    A smart decision, knowing which is which

This special couple were my maternal grandparents
   Jake with the bald spot atop of his head
Laughed and said "Grandma pulled it all out"
   And Laura's hair, never cut, worn in a bun

When Grandpa retired, they moved into town
   And what fun we'd have in the summertime
Grandpa took us on walks and played dominoes
   Grandma did cooking and took us aquiltin'

Jake and Laura, a lifetime of helping others
   He'd help the widows doing little things
She'd take fresh baked goods to the needy
   Together, they helped Mom with everything

I learned a lot from Grandpa and Grandma
   Fairness in playing games, love of reading
"Eat what is set before you and say nothing"
   Made me ashamed of my constant complaining

Looking back, I recall their sense of humor
   I still see Grandpa reading from one eye
And Grandma, so brown, working in the garden
   Or helping Mom bake a cherry or apple pie

— April 6, 1996 —

Fred and Willie

It doesn't seem like twenty years have passed

   Since our friendship with Fred and Millie began

But in 1976, we were all in Marriage Encounter

   We lived nearby so joined the same afterglow

Then I discovered Willie could sign her ABC's

   I thought she was Millie until she spelled Willie

Fred owns Fred's Barber Shop where Mel got haircuts

   Willie was my customer when I was an Avon lady

Willie was staying at her aunt's farm in Chesaning

   When she met Fred on a neighborly Sunday visit

It was the 1940's and World War II was raging on

   At his parent's farm, Fred's input was important

Father Henry, Fred's first cousin, a new priest

   Performed the wedding ceremony on June 10th, 1944

At St. Michael's Catholic Church in New Lothrop

   All's O.K. Fred and Willie have been wed 50 and more

Fred was inducted into the army in April of 1945

   But saw his first son, Jim, born before boot camp

God blessed Fred and Willie with six lovely children

   Six joys being Jim, Jerry, Joel, Kathy, Bob and Ken

Chesaning was their home for the first sixteen years

   Then they moved their little family to Clio in 1960

Just before their fortieth anniversary in May of 1984

   God took Jim Home as he coached Little League

For years Fred and Willie had an unusual family group

   There were the same number of sons and grandsons

And just one daughter and granddaughter, you see

   And then twins, one more granddaughter and grandson

Fred and Willie have been together over half a century

   Fred still runs his barber shop three days a week

Willie is a volunteer at the Clio Convalescent Center

   And she and I go on Communion calls every other week

Fred and Willie have enjoyed traveling to many places

   And especially had a unique time visiting Germany

I often see them out walking here and there about town

   Or along the bike path enjoying the beautiful scenery

Here's to many more "Golden Years"

A Tribute to Brenda

Just a little over a year ago this February
    Mary came to the laundry room to inform me
We finally had a new activities director
    Would I like to go down and meet Brenda Schafer?

Brenda stepped right in and won our hearts
    With her beautiful welcoming smile to start
Her ideas were to get to know everyone
    And discover our interests, true and simple

From crossword puzzles to field trips
    Along with all the parties and potlucks
On through arts and crafts in the activities room
    Right on down to pet therapy once a month

If you needed to cry, her arms were there
    For Brenda is full of love, to give and share
Time flies and she is leaving a short year later
    For a new job at the Clio Convalescent Center

We're going to miss Brenda at Pine Creek Manor
    For as the saying goes, "Our loss is their gain"
But with thankful hearts and loving gratitude
    We all join in to wish the best for Brenda

February 21, 1996

John and Alice Kertesz

It seems like yesterday, not two years ago
    That I first met Alice in the laundry room
Then I noticed they were at the weekly Masses
    They came for the Rosary, and Alice lectured

John is from Michigan, Alice from Wisconsin
    He was an autoworker at Buick in Flint
She was a certified one room school teacher
    Summers, she worked at jobs she could find

Our country was in the midst of World War II
    When John met Alice in the summer of '43
John Kertesz wed Alice Gomashek October 5th
    A beautiful Indian summer day at 75°

John and Alice raised three lovely daughters
    Barbara grew up to become a psychologist
Theresa writes computer software manuals
    And Mary cares for people as a nurse

John and Alice are proud grandparents also
    Of Christopher, Daniel, Rachel and Amy
They've done a lot working and playing together
    Two sweethearts for over half a century

John retired and they moved to Pine Creek Manor
    Where the Clio Bike Path is at their door
And on lovely days, you'll see them walking
    Enjoying the sunshine and getting exercise

John and Alice are enjoying retirement fully
    They're active in the Senior Citizens Center
Enjoying the country is a treasured pastime
    Along with reading, praying, being together

They've traveled far on a lifetime journey
    Their favorites are Arizona and California
I still run into Alice in the laundry room
    A sunny smile and a warm bear hug awaiting me

Best of health for years and years to come

Mary Jekel

My acquaintance with Mrs. Jekel goes way back
   To when I was a Freshman at Clio High School
Mrs. Jekel was my physical education teacher
   And that was over thirty years ago, too

If we had just walked in physical education
   I'm sure I would have been a model student
But we played ball and took all those tests
   Mrs. Jekel was a good, understanding teacher

Mary met Edward Jekel in Great Falls, Montana
   Just before the end of World War II in 1945
Edward Jekel married Mary LaFaun Kulcinski
   On a snowy Easter Sunday, April 1st, 1945

Mary went to college in LaCrosse and Madison, WI
   And her teaching career spanned thirty years
Twenty-one of which were in the Clio Area Schools
   She retired in 1978 at the end of the school year

Edward and Mary raised four lovely children
    Mary Helen, Donald, Barbara and Richard John
They traveled the country over from sea to sea
    Mary says "There's no place like home, the USA"

Mary stayed very active in sports for many years
    And even took a scenic ten day bicycle trip
Traveling from seventy to ninety miles each day
    Along the shore of Maryland to North Carolina

Mary has been retired for eighteen years now
    And daily goes to the Thetford Senior Center
She enjoys reading, knitting and playing euchre
    And it is an honor to write about my teacher

Back then she was Mrs. Jekel, now it's just Mary
    We both call Pine Creek Manor our home now
And enjoy many Saturday afternoon euchre games
    How fast time flies by and how small the world

Shirley

It was Grandpa Hiller's fifty-ninth birthday
    And it was also Monday, Labor Day in 1946
When Shirley Ann Karner entered the world
    The oldest child of Frank and Irene Karner

Our grandfather's name was Jacob Jesse Hiller
    He'd love to pass Jesse to his granddaughter
But there was a beautiful piano player at church
    Irene admired and named her daughter after her

Shirley is my sister, only 359 days older than I
    But circumstances made her grow up much faster
The entire family had the whooping cough in 1952
    And I was very sick with encephalitis and fever

Shirley became "the little mom" though sick, too
    She learned to clean house and wash the dishes
Mom was very sick and could not help her much
    But Shirley came through and she was only six

I can't recall her climbing trees, making mud pies
    Getting into mischief or playing in the haymow
It seems like she was always "Mom's Little Helper"
    And did her very best to ease Mom's heavy load

Naturally, Shirley enjoyed playing house and school
    With Paula Marsh, Barb Bowns and Fran Romanack
When she became a teenager, she was well prepared
    All those babysitting jobs were done with pride

Shirley was in the Clio High School Marching Band
    And played her clarinet with pride at the games
She graduated with honors in the "Class of '65"
    On October 19th, 1968, she became Mrs. Ray Harris

Shirley works at The University of Michigan, Flint
    And is the proud mother of Scott and Carrie
On April 6th, 1994, she became a doting grandma
    To the cutest little granddaughter, Ashley

I am so proud to write this cute little verse
    About my loving sister who is turning fifty
Shirley's been someone to look up to over the years
    And I hope the years ahead are special and nifty

July 10, 1996

I'm Glad

I'm glad I made a difference in someone's life

He needed me, he wanted me, He loved me so

Why he answered my ad nearly three years ago

Only the Lord above, the reason will ever know

His name was Lewis and he'd write every day

And his dialogue was mostly of his love for me

How glad I am to have enriched his last days

For he said we'd be together until eternity

He was in a bad place, he'd done some wrong

But I never gave up hope, he'd turn to the right

For we must remember, we're all the Lord's people

We can turn sadness to joy, darkness to light

Although we can't believe everything he'd said,

   The love he felt for me was etched on his face

I knew without a doubt, it was the real thing

   These are the memories I'll always embrace

We were brought together for a reason, I'm sure

   And I'm glad I took the time to be nice and write

The time always flew by fast on our visits together

   He would make me laugh and we knew we were right

Yesterday, a letter came back marked "deceased"

   Lewis, who'd turned sixty-three the last of June

Nearly a week before had gone to his eternal rest

   And I'm glad I knew him until his final tune

In loving memory

My Thoughts

I just can't seem to concentrate much tonight

I thought I'd write about my old school

But my mind seems to do whatever it might

Do you think that's cool, or not so cool?

One thing for sure, everyone makes mistakes

We have to learn from them as we go along

They let us know if we have what it takes

Are we going to cry or sing an old song?

I think I'll put my pen aside and go to bed

My eyes don't want to stay awake tonight

Besides, it might just help clear my head

Maybe in the morn, I can draw a fright

Monday morning has disappeared to the past

Afternoon is here and my tiredness, too

How I do long for a good old winter's nap

I'd love to waken and find no more snow

We are all handicapped to some degree

There's no such thing as a perfect person

Unaided, most of us can walk and hear and see

But each still has their own limitation

Another sure thing, our Lord isn't choosy

He loves us — mistakes, limitations and all

There's absolutely no reason to feel lousy

Accept yourself with grace and stand tall

God's Beauty

Take a look out the window
And see the sun all aglow
The flowering trees blooming
Mother Earth is rebirthing!

The birds are building nests
And noisy frogs croak loudest
Honeybees go about their duties
And God created these beauties!

The beautiful picture outside
Was created by God's Pride
For only He could master this
The painting so glorious!

The air is scented with spring
With God's loving and caring
He gave each flower a fragrance
And such beauty in a glance!

The sky has different hues
    Of the most beautiful blues
And clouds that bring rain
    God created this, it's plain!

The wind brings forth breezes
    That gently sway the trees
There's coolness in the shade
    And rest in the grassy glade

Farmers will be planting crops
    And each seed split the tops
Each plant knowing what to do
    Because God made it grow!

When you hear the birds chirp
    Or see a scampering chipmunk
Rest under the star studded sky
    Know that God is working high!

April 28, 1998

Pine Creek Manor

We're right behind the Clio Square Shopping Center

    We've got the beautiful Clio Bike Path at our door

This building has an east wing and a west wing to it

    'Tis our home by the Pine Run Creek; Pine Creek Manor

And the people within these walls, all different, unique

    Herbie enjoys playing checkers every now and then

Bea lives under me, says we're quiet as can be up here

    Glenna, on the second floor, west wing, sells her Avon

I live in 313 on the east wing and Jill lives in 313 West

    Very interesting, Jill and I both know sign language

There is Joe and Jane, and also, John and Alice, couples

    With over half a century to their name of marriage

Down near the corner is the home of John and Marie

    She works in the kitchen, his beard's white as snow

Don Kaake moved in early this year on the first floor

    He's always got stories or goodies to share, you know

If you are lucky to always be a winner, never a loser

    Then you can be positive, that has to be Winnie

There's someone else here on the third floor who writes

    I am her strength, but she's my own dear Minnie

George and Mildred have their beautiful cat, Pugsley

    And Eunice and Andres have their service dog, Pepper

This place is well taken care of by Brett and Lance

    We also have Mary, the nicest, sweetest housekeeper

There's Paula Shaw, our manager, who makes things right

    Someone here is always playing cards, euchre or 31

Lots of residents enjoy bingo on Tuesday and Friday night

    Birthdays are celebrated one Saturday afternoon a month

In '62-'63, Mary Jekel was my Physical education teacher

    Oh, I wish I could name everyone in this little poem

Everyone is a special neighbor in their own little way

    I enjoy all the friendship in my "home sweet home"

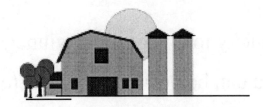

Childhood Memories

I am a farmer's daughter from Clio, Michigan
  And I remember planting, growing and harvest
There was always plenty of work to be done
  But there was also fun, mischief and rest

Of course, we were forbidden to play in the haymow
  But what a grand old time we'd have up there
Then, there was that old box elder "tip top" tree
  Its branches spread just right for a seat upstairs

Two garages did we have with a bar between the two
  Attached to the light post, it made a perfect seat
Many times in childhood, Larry was my companion
  As we trudged the irrigation ditch or played tag

When our friends and playmates came for a good time
We'd play barefoot tag, of which I was fastest
Or our wide sidewalk was the scene for playing catch
That was a favorite game when Bruce came to visit

Oh, those sweet bees in the hot corn and bean fields
But the weeds had to be pulled and the beans hoed
When the combining of wheat and oats was all finished
We'd find plenty of grasshoppers in the "gold"

Haymowing seemed to be Larry's least favorite chore
It was hot, muggy work, but not for us four girls
We'd follow that hay mower and always get in the way
But the best part was the high ride on the hay

Helping Mom with the gardening, freezing and canning
We learned quite a bit about preserving for winter
And all those homemade goodies sure were delicious
Jelly, pear honey, tomatoes, pickles and cucumbers

Corn fields make the most wonderful hiding places
   For how can you be found when the stalks are so tall?
The pond hidden in the woods was a good swimming hole
   We'd sneak off to get cool until we heard Mom's call

Chickens, pigs, and cows were raised beside the crops
   And we had Bootsie, our doggie, rescued by us kids
Black with white feet, she'd jump and catch her popcorn
   And she enriched our lives for twelve years, she did

I still remember the poison ivy patch down "cow lane"
   Learning to ride a two wheeled bicycle at fifteen,
Playing hide and go seek in the darnedest of places,
   And following the hay mower with no water canteen

Many things have changed since Mom and Dad moved in
   To their one hundred acre farm nearly fifty years ago
The taxes have skyrocketed and Hurd Road is now paved
   They no longer farm, the Walthers their potatoes grow

September 2, 1996

Janet

Sitting in the hospital room visiting my dear mom
 My thoughts tend to wander, here, there, everywhere
Sometimes, it would be nice to hear the conversation
 But my thoughts are my very own treasures to share

Janet has shown us all what a gem she truly can be
 A daughter, a sister, a mother, a friend and nurse.
How she does those long crazy hours is a real mystery
 But do them she does, it's all in a life's course

Janet works twelve hour shifts as a registered nurse
 But whenever Mom and Dad need her, they just ask
And without much further ado, she'll be on her way
 For family comes first and it's all in the task

Born Janet Kay Karner on a cold February 10th, 1952
 She's my sister, the middle of the "Karner Bunch"
And growing up, she would dream about owning a horse
 But Dad's thinking was they cost too darn much

I recall Janet helping Uncle John with the milking
 When the heavy milk machinery was something new

She'd be out there first thing in the early morning
    Rain or shine, it was the last chore after school

I'm sure all those chores must have prepared her
    For the future hard work of her life's career
Janet also has the most wonderful personality
    And was crowned homecoming queen her senior year

Janet was married to Tom Ward for quite a few years
    And is the mom of two daughters, Kristen and Torre
Now Janet is married to Gary, a great music teacher
    Whom she met at a Nanci meeting in Oklahoma City

Janet's hair is turning silver gray faster than mine
    Four years younger than I, she's not yet a grandma
Her hair will already be gray and she'll look the part
    When her special moment comes to be called Grandma

There are special sisters all over the universe
    But none can ever compare to my three sisters
Shirley, Janet and Karen, the best the Lord sent
    And my heart can recall the sweetest of memories

September 25, 1996

Charles and Audrey Hooks

Not so long ago, it was announced at a Weekly Mass

Charlie Hooks was in the hospital and very ill

He needed our love and prayers to get him through

The Good Lord heard for Charlie is with us still

Charles Willie Hooks was born down south in Missouri

And came to Flint as a small boy in the year 1932

The "Great Depression" was on and jobs were scarce

But Charlie's father found work at General Motors

Audrey Marie Belanger was born in Flint, Michigan

And moved to Pine Run when she was a little girl

She was born the oldest of nine children in 1927

And grew up helping her mother whenever she could

Charlie and Audrey are both from big, loving families

   He had six sisters and James, his one and only brother

Charlie was next to the youngest sibling in his family

   She had a sister, Cecelia, followed by seven brothers

Audrey was cleaning Charlie's sister's kitchen in 1947

   When she met Charlie and their two year courtship began

The wedding took place in Mt. Morris on April 23, 1949

   At St. Mary's Catholic Church performed by Fr. Gannon

After a beautiful reception given by her parents at home

   Charlie took his bride and they started life in Flint

He had a good job with Michigan Bell Telephone Company

   And God sent three children, Vandalie, Mark and Keith

When their three youngsters grew up enough to enjoy golf

   Charlie and Audrey took them on many golfing trips

Golfing trips quickly became a favorite family pastime

    And I know Charlie still has his old golfing spirit

Indeed, Charlie and Audrey are a very special twosome

    And they've worked side by side almost half a century

They have opened their beautiful hearts and home to all

    From the tiny little babies to their own loving family

They have enjoyed many trips to California and Arizona

    When Charlie retired, their winters were in Florida

For thirty years, Audrey did her ceramics to give away

    Now together, they make rosaries for gifts and missions

My prayer is for God to tenderly care for them always

    And enrich them even more through the "Golden Years"

The Clio Bike Path

The Clio Bike Path is right outside the Manor door
And on lovely days when the warm sun is shining
I take that stroll for it's worth the little energy
A friend or two I may see out walking and enjoying

I've walked that path often myself, or with a friend
The beauty striking me anew each and every stroll
I've often seen some little creature run across my path
But not being able to name it makes me wonder somehow

But there are many things I can enjoy as I stroll along
The wind whistling in my ear, the birds' sweet song
Trees along the way with their different hues of green
The sky so blue amid the leaves. I can't be wrong

The bike path goes uphill, over bridges, through tunnels
And all the way the Pine Run Creek goes babbling by
How often have I stopped to watch the waters rushing on
Or to hear the noisy frogs croaking in their haven?

Some days it'll seem like there's no one there but me
That's a special time for prayer and my own pondering
And I know somehow for it seems there's nothing but nature
I never walk the path alone for the Lord is watching

The dancing patches of sunlight through the great trees
Go hither and yon, here and there along the sidewalk
On the hottest, muggiest summer days, I'll feel so cool
As I go strolling through the naturally cool tunnels

The Clio Bike Path goes over six miles through the woods
A canopy of leaves softly forming a bridge overhead
The train may go choo chooing by for the tracks are there
And children with bikes, rollerblades and skateboards

Many of us take the Clio Bike Path for granted these days
However, I can recall when it first started in the park
The City Fathers kept buying more land and adding on
And as long as it's there, I'll enjoy it on the mark

More Childhood Memories

Some of the sweetest memories are those of yesteryear
    And it just seems so natural to write it all down
Born in 1947, I have been a Clio girl my entire life
    It has changed in fifty years from country to town

When I was growing up on our one hundred acre farm
    Our neighborhood had a few houses here and there
Hurd Road was ruts and mudholes every single spring
    And in the wintertime, no salt trucks ever came by

My favorite pastime was curling up with a good book
    A real bookworm, everyone thought I was so quiet
However, I could be just as noisy as anyone else
    Oh yes, my way was always the one I wanted to get

I remember the little blonde walking doll I got at ten
    I named my doll Betty and she was first of her kind
Betty could bend her knees and crawl with my help
    And Grandpa Hiller made her a little white doll bed

One winter when it snowed and snowed and it was high
    Larry, Janet and I made our one and only snow fort
It was so long, it took up a good deal of the yard
    Then what fun we five "Eskimos" had that winter

Directly across the road, there was only the woods
    Where we kids found a tree with a carved rosary
Probably some Indians had carved it years before
    We carved our initials and it was a sacred tree

In town, there were Shethelm and Harris Rexall Drugs
    There was Pettit's, Don's Bootery and Ray's Toggery
Neeland's Hardware Store was located on North Mill St.
    There were Babcock's IGA and Schaupp's Clio Bakery

Mom worked at The Clio State Bank, the only one in town
    Clio was mainly a thriving farming community back then
And The Houghton Elevator was one of the busiest in town
    We went with Dad when he took in the beans and corn

On Saginaw in Pine Run, there was a Wonder Bread Store
   Where Mom bought ten loaves of bread for a dollar
On the southwest corner of Saginaw and Vienna Roads
   We could buy Penny candy at Fairy's little store

Lawrence and Margie Beaune built a house down the road
   They had a little girl, Eleanor, and a dog, Dippy
Margie made beautiful birthday cakes for the Karners
   She was 4-H leader and taught artistic embroidery

Some things stand out much better in memory than others
   I still hear Dad's "Always do the very best you can"
Margie used to say "Slow down and take smaller steps"
   And curled up cozy with a good book, my companion

The Wall in the Aisle

Why is that "wall" down the main aisle
    If we say "The Our Father" together
And ask the Lord to erase feelings of ill
    Shouldn't we all be united in prayer?

That "wall" tumbled down at Christmas
    And it also crumbles at Eastertime,
But isn't our Lord here at every Mass?
    Why then don't we unite all the time?

Come then, one parish family all together
    Don't be afraid to unite across the hall,
Join hands and recite, "The Our Father",
    Unity and love will mean no more "wall"

Friends and Neighbors

We'd been waiting all summer, and it was December 1973
   When we moved our family from Field Road to Roseberry
Our youngest, Brian, had turned three the week before
   Thanksgiving was over and Christmas fast approaching

By then, Mel and I had been married for over seven years
   Besides Brian, we had two daughters; Melinda and Tammy
On one side in the brown house, Ron and Karen moved in
   And the off-white house was home to Fran and Johnny

Our first January on Roseberry Lane, it snowed and snowed
   Karen, Fran and Jenny came over and we got acquainted.
One day feeling a little brave, I bundled the kids up warm
   And we plowed a pathway through the deep snow to Karen's

Snowy January 1974 was the start of a lasting friendship
   Of the Ronald Stanbaugh and Malcolm Grindel families
Mel and I had our three children, six, four and three
   In 1976 and 1977, Ron and Karen had two new babies

Friends, we did much together for the next twenty years,

    Worked together and watched each other's children grow

Played scrabble, hearts, canasta, euchre and horseshoes

    And if we needed something, we knew where to borrow

And it never, never mattered what we needed in the least

    A cup of sugar, coffee, an onion, tools or lawnmower

Our friendship was always based on respect and trust

    We helped each other any way we could, here and there

In 1983, Karen was going to have another baby, a girl

    Our friend, Phyllis, and I joined our heads together

We invited Karen and her friends to a Tupperware Party

    But the nicest "Tupperware Party" was a baby shower

Over the years, we enjoyed many picnics and fireworks

    The Clio Merchants had a rock-athon one hot summer

We all encouraged Mel and Doctor Carter sponsored him

    He fell asleep, but he put up the greatest effort

It seems we were always planting new trees and flowers

    Roses, white birch, snowball bushes, lilacs and maple

When Tammy was five, she and Robbie went into the woods

    And Mel planted the little box elder she had pulled

The Stanbaughs and Grindels, friends from Vienna Woods

    Never missed a chance to compare notes after Halloween

To see just how many trick-or-treaters we had that night

    It was always over the one hundred mark for our team

Mel is in Heaven now and I have the sweetest memories

    Our kids have grown up and Meghan is now a teenager

Ryan and Derek are working and I have moved to town

    And Ron and Karen will soon celebrate their silver

Neal

Sitting in the library so quiet
　　I'm wondering what to write
Always, I feel the Lord so near
　　And there's Neal sitting at my right

A beautiful man that God created
　　So sensitive and caring to my needs
He's reading *USA Today* for he can see
　　And I'm sitting thinking of his deeds

Neal takes my hand so I don't tumble
　　Lets me know when there are stairs
At the zoo, he pointed out the birds
　　These are some ways he shows he cares

A precious man, his hearing has gone
　　It's hard to make him understand
He's trying his best to learn to sign
　　Someday he'll be able to comprehend

Born Neal Dayne Hausmann on May 3rd, 1951
　　He's the son of a Baptist minister
Little children make his eyes sparkle so
　　A feat I just can't seem to master

Neal's lucky he can see, it comes in handy
　　And he can depend on the written word
So count his blessings each day, he must
　　He'll trust the Lord and look forward

August 15, 1997

To Sunny California

My son, Brian and I flew West to Los Angeles, California
    To Deaf Expo '96 and the plane landed right on time
The stars twinkled above and the music made my feet dance
    Flying hands were everywhere and I knew I was no prime

I can't remember ever seeing oranges growing on trees
    But there outside the window, I saw some growing away
The beautiful mountains along the way to the Deaf Expo
    I just couldn't help singing about this wondrous day

Monday we spent seven hours getting lost in Disneyland
    Brian and I agreed, we liked Splash Mountain the best
Followed by the haunted mansion of horrible creatures
    We got help to the exit and four days to see the rest

We spent most of Tuesday where Mickey lives in Toon Town
    And had foot long hotdogs and chips at Pluto's Doghouse
Donald Duck gave me a nice hug and his "big beak" kiss
    And we were photographed with our star, Mickey Mouse

Brian decided to try the pool at the Hampton Inn Wednesday
    The water was perfect and we left later than usual
We spent a lot of time on underground rides that fair day
    And liked Pirates Cruise where dead men tell no tales

The tunnel of Alice in Wonderland is so very beautiful
    The ride in Roger Rabbit's spinning cars made me dizzy
I can hardly believe winter is coming and November is here
    The Southern California days are sunny, warm and breezy

By the fourth day, we felt like old pros around Disneyland
    And had no trouble at all finding our way from end to end
We rode the Jolly Trolley and upstairs in the green Omnibus
    Brian said we'd walked fifty miles and my feet agreed

Friday found my poor, aching feet complaining bitterly
    And I was ready and willing for a wheelchair tour
We went on all our favorite rides again; the spaceship
    Splash Mountain, Peter Pan's Flight and little cars

Disneyland is full of wonderful acts of human kindness
    The young man who helped me find just the right sizes
A lady arranged a shortcut to a ride so I wouldn't fall
    The worker who steered us toward the exit for the bus

Saturday morning found us starting on an eight hour tour
  Through Beverly Hills, Hollywood and Farmer's Market
We saw the names, footprints and handprints of the stars
  And I ate the best food of the week, a turkey burger

Those kindnesses of the wonderful people at Hampton Inn
  Made our stay in Anaheim, California a trip to remember
We know they went beyond the call of duty and services
  And we'll always be grateful to them, forever and ever

Kimberly Renaud

Kim, Robin and Libby, I met in March
During my first week in Kalamazoo
And I was curious if they knew ASL
They knew some and played Skip Bo

Kim stopped to talk to Neal and me
And she'd been here thirteen weeks
She'd been blind for eight months
A pretty blond with rosy cheeks

Her apartment was across the hall
And she'd stop by to talk and rap
Or to tell me it was lunch time
I'd even read her poetic scrap

Kim has always lived near Detroit
And is a wife and mom in Clawson
On a rainy December 4th in 1993
James Renaud wed Kimberly Hinton

Kim says when it rains on weddings
"It's tears of heavenly happiness"
And brings good luck, a good omen
What a nice way to spread gladness

Jim and Kim have two cute children
Christopher James on October 14, 1993
And Breanna Nacole born June 19,1996
That's a very special little family

Kim studied for a year at college
And worked at good customer service
Now she's blind and training afresh
She'll succeed cuz she's so nice

Kim has green eyes, her favorite color
And she loves crafts, music and dance
Jim works as a data mail truck driver
And here's hope for joy and happiness!

My Feelings About Jim

Jim's first call on September 6th seemed like the start
    Of something that could lead to a lasting friendship
We talked and talked for a while and ran up the phone bill
    He said he was afraid, he'd been hurt in relationships

Jim said he wanted to be friends first, which made sense
    There are two thousand miles between my home and his
And Jim said I was welcome to share his humble abode
    When I read in the "Silent News" about Deaf Expo '96

However, Jim's welcome was the shortest I've ever known
    His actions spoke, he'd made up his mind ahead of time
And there was no food in the apartment, nothing at all
    I was lucky to have my Nanci which I took at bedtime

I explained to him I wanted first of all companionship
    And he had made me a promise, he'd stay by my side
But he left us at the Deaf Expo to find our own way
    When he drove, it was on a ninety mile an hour ride

Brian, sitting in the back, could read his speedometer
   He was bouncing back there, couldn't read the signs
I firmly believe in the love of our Lord and Saviour
   And my special Guardian Angel, who works overtime

I just don't understand, Jim can tease but can't be teased
   And he was ready to send us home before we wanted to go
I couldn't talk to him, he doesn't seem to listen to reason
   He dropped us at Disneyland's Door, I'm thankful to know

My faith and trust in men has been shattered anew again
   And I'm about ready to concede, there are no more good men
Really and truly, I don't understand where I fit into things
   I'm not deaf and I can't hear, I'm somewhere in between

Those oranges were growing outside Jim's kitchen window
   On the way to the Expo we saw some California scenery
The beautiful mountains were there, and the day so warm
   I wish I could have taken some California home with me

Twenty-Six

You're twenty-six, my son
No longer a little boy
I have the fondest memories
Of how you relished every toy

But now, you're twenty-six
A man, five feet eleven
I want you to know, I love you
For I understand you even

But you must remember
I am your mother
You could do a few little extras
To make life easier

If you make a mess
Clean it up
Sleep between the sheets
You'll warm the bed up

Don't leave the chips open
They tend to get stale
I'm tired, wash the dishes
If you help, you'll not fail

I'm thankful to have a son
Who is as special as you
But sometimes I can't believe you're twenty-six
You really seem more like two

Your dad has gone to Heaven
And one day, I'll be gone
We're only on earth for a while
You're twenty-six, you're a man grown

I love you for the kindness you show
For being you as only you can be
You are strong, I love your strength
And I love you when you worry

Thirteen years ago, you became a teenager
That's half your life ago, now you're twenty-six
I love you because you're a special son
And I hope you enjoy being twenty-six

Happy 26th Birthday, Brian
I love you

What Earthly Reason

As I sit here with my pen in hand
    Lord, help me always to understand

Just what earthly reason I must have
    For being me, for the unique way I am

I am deaf, but I can hear You, Lord
    You talk to me and I can hear Your Word

I can feel You forever near at hand
    Do come to me, Lord, and help me stand

Seeing can be very hard, but I surely can
    I can see You in the heart of the land

All the earthly goodness comes from love
    The Lord bestowed on us from above

The Lord has been there through the ages
    In big and little things life engages

He's there in blowing wind and stormy sea
    But most of all, He's there in you and me

God is our Lord, the Lord is wondrous love
    Spread His Word, enriched by Him above

The Lord is in my heart and ready smile
    He's there every step, every single mile

Maybe I can assure you of my earthly reason
    To tell you the Lord is here every season

His beautiful love is there for everyone
    The bold, the sick, the weak and strong

A Longing in My Heart

There's a longing in my heart for thee
   For my honey who has gone to Eternity

I'll always remember how wonderful you were
   And it seems the pain will always be there

As the years go rolling on, I recall
   Just how nice you were, the best of all

I remember those daily calls at one from work
   You just wanted to make sure I was OK

Mel, always lending a helping hand
   In more ways than one, my right hand man

I miss you, Sweetheart, so very often
   Your "I love you's" were so important

Oh Mel, we blossomed together as one
   But the tears come, my better half is gone

I was nineteen and you were twenty-two
    When at Saints Charles and Helena, we said "I do"

You were a bashful young man back then
    My encouragement helped you to the man within

I think your last days will always be
    Forever etched in my heart and memory

I wanted to be a clown in the parade
    And of course, you joined me, my comrade

You wanted to sell tickets, the loyal usher
    For our church, always the dependable wonder

But, Mel, my sweet, you weren't feeling well
    That heart attack left memories to dwell

Almost twenty-five years we had, you and me
    It wasn't enough, my heart still longs for thee

December 9, 1996

George and Mildred Hollenback

This freezing morning, I looked outside my window

    At the sparkling diamonds in the fresh fallen snow

And my thoughts turned to a beautiful December bride

    Long ago in 1951 with George Hollenback by her side

George was an air force sergeant from Mount Clemens

    And Mildred worked in a stove factory in the 1940's

And that's how these sweethearts met, the two of them

    When George was discharged, Buick in Flint hired him

George Joseph Hollenback wed Mildred Elizabeth Meyers

    Two days before Christmas at St. Mary's in Mt. Morris

The ceremony was performed by Father Frederick Horton

    After giving Mildred instructions in Catholic doctrine

In 1954, George and Mildred purchased their little house

Out on North Elms Road at the western boundary of Clio

Little children warmed their hearts and they had to share

So they took in premature babies and did foster care

Finally in 1961, George and Mildred adopted Theresa Marie

A precious little daughter who made their lives merry

Following in her parent's footsteps with a loving heart,

She grew up loving children and works in foster care

In church, George and Mildred always sit in the last pew

George is a dedicated member of K of C and also the VFW

Mildred enjoyed knitting and crocheting for many years

United, they made a home through good times and tears

The two of them enjoy practicing their Catholic beliefs

He was an usher for years and helped at the breakfasts

For seventeen years, she taught little children in CCD

    They also helped with Vincent de Paul and food pantry

George, Mildred and Pugsley moved to Pine Creek Manor

    When housekeeping got to be a bit much in summer, 1994

I was surprised to see them downstairs at donut hour

    But then we got into some Saturday games of euchre

This year has not been very kind to George and Mildred

    At the doctor's office, she fell and broke her shoulder

Later she broke her hip and George had pneumonia, wow

    And our love and prayers will surely help them now

Now, here it's forty-five years since their "I do's"

    That's four decades plus five, as everyone knows

A long, long time of giving, loving and sharing as one

    And here's hoping God will make '97 a better one

January Birthdays

For sure, January birthdays have something special
   They ring in a whole new year, besides the usual

Pine Creek Manor has nine birthdays in January
   I know most of these folks, but not everybody

Tom Tawfiq is the very first to celebrate his day
   Cuz he rings it right in with New Year's Day

When the year is nine days old, it's Verna Neely
   I pass her in the hall and she likes my poetry

Ann Miller and Marie Simon have to share the eleventh
   Two very nice ladies, I believe, for I know both

The next day belongs to Joe Ghazale, my neighbor
   A nice man, he seems, but I see him next to never

The fifteenth has a memory of someone very dear
   My youngest sister, Karen, who never lived here

Alice Kertesz and Robert Grimm share the eighteenth
   And they are from the third floor, west wing

Martin Luther King, Jr. Day is the third Monday
　　He died for civil rights, now it's a holiday

The twentieth is also special for Helen Borowski
　　She's from floor three and works doing laundry

Just before the month of January has its ending
　　There's another birthday for lovely Lola Worthing

Seven January birthdays from Pine Creek Manor
　　Are from way up here on the very top floor

Hilton Miller married Ann Knapp on December first
　　Their hearts with happiness and joy do burst

When Brian and I first moved to Pine Creek Manor
　　It was Marie Simon who invited us to donut hour

Martin Luther King and Karen have gone to heaven
　　But they made their mark and are not forgotten

Yes, January is a beginning of a brand new year
　　And we wish the very best to those we hold dear

December 30, 1996

Five Jerks

The inspiration for this ditty about jerks

    Was prompted by my good friend, Jill

I tend to confide in her about everything

    She said to write about the jerks as well

The first jerk was Jack from Mackinaw City

    He was my childhood sweetheart in the 1950's

We went to our twenty-fifth class reunion

    And had some good dances and old memories

But Jack is afraid in the world of women

    He has spent most of this life as a bachelor

He made me pay for his wine on Mackinaw Island

    Ordered flowers for my grandson, not paid for

Jerk number two was a big man named Thomas

   He lived in Flint and was janitor at MSD

We met through a teacher who also worked there

   But Tom wanted one thing, I said "No way"

A short, fun man named Ed was number three

   He wormed his way into our trusting hearts

Mom and Dad asked for his help on the farm

   And he did little things for us from the start

We discovered in the end, he was a born liar

   He said he had cancer to get our sympathy

He seemed trustworthy, returned what he borrowed

   Then slicker than slick, he took our money

The *Flint Journal* ran a weekly "Companion Column"

   My ad was answered by Lew, the fourth jerk

For nearly three years, he held me with lies

    He died and now I know I'm no love expert

Well, there's only one more, that'll make five

    This time, it was a personal ad in *Silent News*

I answered his ad and he called from California

    Jim's his name and he was missing some screws

Each of these jerks, a breed of his very own

    But none had the makings of a true friendship

He has to be a Christian, tell the honest truth

    Then we'll be on our way to a lasting relationship

Anyway, I'll keep looking forward to the future

    Maybe the Good Lord will find him somewhere

Someone who likes to dance and enjoy a good time

    My standards are high, but he's out there

February

Before I begin this little verse about February
    I admit to missing two birthdays in January

Sunday, January nineteenth was Hilda Barrett's
    The mother of Jean, one of my former classmates

The twenty-second belonged to "retired" Don Dyer
    I saw the birthday greeting over his office door

Groundhog Day is always the second day of February
    Hopefully, he'll come and tell spring to hurry

We have two different Ollies in our Manor Community
    They both celebrate their birthdays in February

My sweet sister, Janet entered the world the tenth
    And this year, she will celebrate her forty-fifth

Angela Labrenz is a very special "February Babe"
    She rings in the twelfth alongside "Honest Abe"

Forget me not the lovely day of hearts and roses
    On Valentine's Day, I send love and sweet verses

Remember George, the chopper of the cherry tree?
    His birthday's the twenty-second and that's no lie

The twenty-fifth, a day for lovely Cecelia Moore
    She lives in The Manor, west wing second floor

George Simpson keeps a deck of cards in his pocket
    Always ready to play, the last day's his ticket

I'd like to remember Vi in this little February poem
    She's sadly missed for God took her quickly Home

It's great, February is the shortest month of the year
    The faster it goes, the sooner spring will be here

Robin

When I think of robins, they're songbirds
    But in Kalamazoo, I've met another kind
This robin is human all the way through
    She's learning to cope with being blind

Can you ever think of a bird having a dog
    Because they are supposed to be enemies?
Well, this must be a new kind of situation
    Robin's dog is Reese and they are cronies

Roberta June Beynon's entrance in 1965
    Was at summer's end, on September first
Robin was the oldest child in her family
    As Charles, her brother, is the youngest

Robin's Dad and Mom, Robert and Audrey
    Have gone to heaven to be with our Lord
She has a very dear sister-in-law, Tammy
    Four nephews and three nieces on record

The yellow rose is Robin's favorite flower
    And she loves food, fresh fruit and pizza
Kalamazoo, Michigan has been home to Robin
    But she has some family living in Georgia

Robin has traveled out west to Disneyland
    And loves the beautiful California weather
She also ventured south to South Carolina
    And saw the country between here and there

Soft peach is the color Robin likes the best
    And she enjoys visiting family and friends
Listening to television and radio is a hobby
    Robin also likes shopping for odds and ends

Teaching Robin sign language was lots of fun
    For it made someone whom I could understand
And I know Robin is full of patience and love
    She'll succeed for she's a good robin brand!

Pine Run School Days – 1950's

I was very sick with encephalitis and fever at age five

    Causing me to miss half of my first kindergarten year

So in September of 1953, I started all over once again

    This made me older than most of my classmates by a year

I have many wonderful memories to cherish of those years

    When I went to Pine Run Elementary School on the hill

From kindergarten forth, there was someone very dear

    A cute little redheaded boy, Jackie, filled the bill

Jackie Zimmerman was always by my side way back then,

    He was raised with the best manners of any classmate

My terrible illness had affected my hearing and eyesight

    But Jackie was my best friend, my favorite playmate

Jackie's Mom, Stella, worked hard in the school kitchen

She and Mrs. Tidball made some really delicious meals

I remember best their mouth-watering goulash and cobbler

Their fish and chips on Fridays and those hot rolls

He had one glass eye and was almost blind in the other

He was the best janitor ever, his name was Al Miller

His laughter and teasing rang true for the youngsters

I recall him sitting on the rail around the fruit cellar

What would school be like without the dedicated teachers?

I can still imagine them at their desks and blackboards

From little Mrs. Moore to Mrs. Anway to Mrs. Richardson

Mrs. Johnson taught 4-H, square dancing and fourth grade

Pine Run School was situated on a sacred green terrace

The back hill was bare and eroded, no grass grew there

Between the two hills were many steps to the playground

At spring recess, these were our "Mother May I?" stairs

Down on the playground were some swings, teeter-totters

    A giant slide and a baseball diamond for playing ball

The gurgling Pine Run Creek rushed through the east side

    The sacred green terrace was not to be walked on at all

Beyond the parking lot was the forbidden, tempting swamp

    There were bushes perfect for playing house and school

Gee, Jackie, Vernon Borrow, Randy Lagatitz, I and others

    Often got lectured for not minding the school rule

Going to school and learning, something I loved to do

    I couldn't hear well, walked to the blackboard to see

When I started third grade, I got a hearing aid from MSD

    That didn't help much except to make the rooms noisy

That dear old school of yesteryear is still standing tall

    Remodeled, senior citizens get together daily upstairs

The Clio branch of the county library is the bottom floor

    Children still slide downhill and the memories are there

February 16, 1997

Lee and Pat Roots

Mel and I had been married one year and three months

    When we bought our first little house on Field Road

Our neighbors on the west side were Lee and Pat Root

    They had four children growing up fast and good

For six short years, we lived side by side as friends

    Until we moved to our brand new house on Roseberry

I recall cutting my hand opening a peanut butter jar

    Pat was helping at my home when her dad died in Perry

In June of 1953, Pat was babysitting for her cousin

    And Lee's niece was watching the neighbor's kids

The babysitters got acquainted, that's how Pat met Lee

    They had a good year's courtship before they were wed

The rites were planned in Pat's aunt and uncle's yard

    The day, June 26, 1954, was rainy so they wed inside

The wedding ceremony was performed by Reverend Johnson

    Ernest Lee Root took Patricia Ann Peabody as his bride

Lee and Pat were blessed with four beautiful children

   Two girls and boys; Marjorie, Michael, Kathryn, Timothy

Lee worked at General Motors Parts, Pat as full time mom

   When we were neighbors, they had a gentle dog, Tiny

Tiny grew up to be a good mannered dog, a collie mixture

   When a puppy, he fit nicely into Lee's shirt pocket

The vet instructed Pat to put Tiny on a low fat diet

   I can remember when Tiny got sprayed by a mad skunk

Pat and Lee's kids were always respectful and helpful

   And we often asked them to babysit our little three

Lee and Pat owned a cottage up north on Bertha Lake

   For eight years enjoying vacations with their family

In 1975, Lee and Pat decided to sell their tiny cottage

   And bought a house to use as a cottage in Farwell

In 1980, with Lee's retirement from General Motors Parts

   They packed up and left Clio, lock, stock and barrel

Eight years ago, in 1989, they moved to Paisley, Florida

    They have nine grandchildren and one great-grandchild

They have a motorhome and enjoy traveling the country

    This year plan to visit the six states in New England

This twosome have come to cherish their Florida home

    They like taking walks, smelling the orange blossoms

Pat sews and crochets, making homemade family treasures

    United, they lead a good life, honest and wholesome

This year, 1997, marks forty-three years of marriage

    Pat and Lee are enjoying retirement to the fullest

They cherish precious time spent with their family

    And seeing this beautiful country from east to west

March

March is really, truly here, winter's at its end

A nice man, Carmen Key, has a birthday the second

    He has to share that date with Mildred Hollenback

    Who is very happy to be home and back on track

The tenth of March is a special day for John Fry

This should make the man smile, he can but try

    On March seventeenth, just before first of spring

    Find a little Leprechaun and do an Irish fling

And don't forget, drink green beer, eat Irish stew

Lift your hat, it's "Top o' the morning to you"

    March the twentieth has a special double meaning

    My brother, Larry, was born first day of spring

Roger Gillam was born the twenty-ninth of March

He and Verna Neely go out and have a sweet touch

I can't think of a better name than Myrtle Buning

Especially if she comes in with the Easter Bunny

Wondrous springtime brings rebirth to Mother Earth

Glorious Easter refreshes our soul, renews faith

Michigan's March is a wonderful miracle to behold

When winter and spring have their battles unfold

It's March so enjoy your springtime to the fullest

Listen to the birds, take walks and be an optimist

Making a New Friend

There was a personal ad in February's *Silent News*
   David, a nice guy, was looking for a special lady
He said he was tall, widowed and liked walking, too
   Traveling was on his list and I thought "maybe"

So I took a chance and wrote to David's box number
   He answered, wrote, and said he was interested
He said his mother, Mary, lived in Cincinnati, Ohio
   Soon he made flight reservations and a car rented

The traffic was good and it didn't take him long.
   David called when he arrived, said he was hungry
I said I'd make him some lunch, I'd love to do it
   He chose tuna instead of turkey, that was a dandy

David is tall, handsome and very nice and I'm so short
   I love to laugh and be merry, he said he was happy
We took a short walk east on the almost dry bike path
   And then visited Mom and Dad because it got rainy

Two days we spent, having such a wonderful good time
    We visited some museums, won a good game of canasta
I got a picture of Roy Rogers and Trigger at Redbeard's
    And David met my grandsons also, Brandon and Joshua

Now, I'm hoping we'll meet again very, very soon
    I've never been to New Jersey, an eastern state
And David would enjoy our museums in the summertime
    Maybe a flame of love will ignite on a future date

My Friend, Noreen

I could never write this book of poems and verse
　Without a special ditty about my friend, Noreen
I love to talk to her through the Michigan Relay
　For she can make me laugh so, she's not serene

When Mel died, our friendship became a common bond
　Noreen was the one who got me started writing
She asked me to write a verse for the church choir
　I said I couldn't, but try telling her anything

Noreen and I had such silly phone conversations
　I'm sure, together, we drove the relay center wild
Laughter mixed with silliness is the best medicine
　I had lost Mel and she had lost Joan Ina, a child

I was enjoying Kalamazoo in the hot summer of 1993
　When we suffered a loss shared, my sister, Karen
Who was very precious to both her family and mine
　Noreen is Karen's husband, Leonard's first cousin

I started this poem about Noreen over four years ago
　But I lost it, and it has never been recovered
And I can't get her to answer any of my questions
　But the first verse was one my mind remembered

Noreen worked at the parish center for many years
    I loved to stop by the office for a hug and chat
But no sooner had I moved to town, than she left
    And got a job elsewhere, now please explain that

My friend, Noreen, has a wonderful sense of humor
    That's what gets her into so much silly trouble
We share a special sweet secret, we're grandmas
    To two grandsons each, that's a blessed double

Rex and Noreen have been married over thirty years
    Two children they had, Alan and Joan Ina Harkins
You know, Noreen was right, I don't need answers
    I know for sure, I wish her the best of everything

I give Noreen a ring whenever I'm down in the dumps
    She never lets me down, the remedy's up her sleeve
Humor does us wonders, we're both naturally silly
    And in the Lord's miracles and goodness, we believe

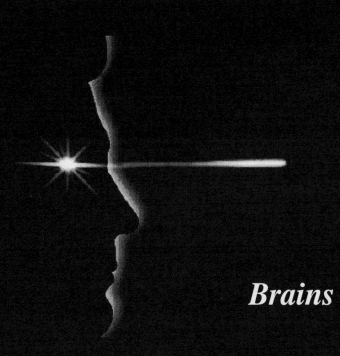

Brains

Brains are like computers much more than we realize
Just think of all the work they do for their size

Your body movements are centered there in the main
It's your brain that lets you know you're in pain

Old memories are stored in the brain's "memory bank"
Good and bad decisions come from the "think tank"

My brain's very good at remembering dates, numbers
Or whatever I need, I'll find it in my "computer"

That childhood phone number is there and it sticks
Murray three-four-one-seven, and, of course, six

I have always counted steps and continue to this day
Just to be safe and sure, I don't stumble the way

In childhood days, I played dominoes with Grandpa
Only scores ending in fives and zeroes added up

It's nineteen years since Sonny left for eternity
Seven-four-three-three-five-five-four, in memory

Here in my Clio home where I dwell, Pine Creek Manor
There are thirty steps between first and third floor

My "human computer" has a special built-in time reflex
Sometimes though, my body is slow when it reacts

The brain is a complex blessing from the Good Lord
So use it wisely and strive to keep His Holy Word

March 2, 1997

Long Time Friends

Mel and I were on a date the weekend before Easter
    It was 1966 and we were at a movie at Northland
Sonny and Freda were also there and talking to Mel
    When I came from the snack room to take his hand

Mel said he hadn't seen Sonny in quite a long time
    Sonny and Freda asked us to their home on Alcott
Mel came and got me Sunday, and we got acquainted
    With them and their three month old baby, Georgia

Sonny and Freda both worked at the Masonic Temple
    In the early 1960's and Sonny popped the question
Darrell Raymond Collins wed Alfreda Beverly Crosier
    In 1963 at First Baptist Church in Flint, Michigan

Darrell was nicknamed Sonny when he was a small tyke
    He and Freda were blessed with two sweet children
Their oldest, Georgia Ann, was born January 12, 1966
    Followed closely by Stephen Wayne on July 21, 1967

We packed a lifetime of friendship into twelve years
Enjoying canasta, going on picnics and camping
Georgia and Stephen hadn't reached their teen years
When in March, 1978, a heart attack claimed Sonny

Sonny worked at General Motors, Chevrolet and Buick
A man he knew and worked with came to his funeral
We were having a picnic in our yard on Roseberry
When Freda came and introduced us to Park Merrill

Park Robert Merrill married Alfreda Crosier Collins
Outside on a lovely, sunny day, September 12, 1981
Mel and I were weekend volunteers at our church fest
And missed the rites but were very happy for them

With a lot of patience, we taught Park to play cards
The amusing thing was, when it wasn't his turn
And even when it was and he had to make a decision
We'd find he'd fallen asleep, he was Mel's partner

Five years ago today, I was at Mom and Dad's house
Recovering from a broken leg that refused to heal

When the unexpected news came by way of the phone
   He'd died quickly in his sleep, our Park Merrill

After Park's death, I lost track of Freda for a time
   Then I found her in a story in the *Flint Journal*
She was at Carriage Town Missions starting all over
   Now she has an office job at C.I., what a finale

Freda is fifty-four and has four sweet grandchildren
   Hardship has been her Taskmaster over the years
My hat is off to her for trying and making the grade
Our Lord has blessed her, washing away her fears

April

I'm silly, I'm foolish, I can't stop my laughter
   But the joke's on me, so join in the banter

For April Fool's Day, I was expecting some snow
   So Mother Nature put a lovely day out my window

I called Dorothy King to wish her a happy birthday
   But her line was busy, um, it's April Fool's Day

Divine sweet pea is flower for the month of April
   Marie Klepplinger rings in with her sweet spell

My friend, Sandy, was born back first on April 4, 1947
   During Flint's Great Flood, two historic events

April 4th, I think, is Hilton Miller's eighty-fifth
   Then there's George Hollenback, his birthday's next

The first Sunday in April, be sure and switch ahead
   The hour will be later so don't plan to stay abed

The seventeenth was the birthday of my darling, Mel
He made it to forty-seven, how I miss him still

Rosie whom I met in Kalamazoo in the summer of 1993
Her day's also the seventeenth, a grandma like me

Mel used to go around the yard with me every April
Showing me the new buds God had started to unfurl

"Your Ride" has finally started throughout the county
But it'd be nice without the complications, you see

Warmer, longer days, I'm really glad it's finally here
April, a time of miracles, here, there, everywhere

The Others

There are many new faces mixed in with familiar ones
At the Michigan Commission for the Blind Training Center
Upon returning to Kalamazoo, Bob was the first I met in March
He's from Flint and has known Melinda, my daughter

Bob used to work at Michigan School for the Deaf
And he is very good at American sign language
He seems to do a little bit of everything,
Working the starlight shift and a substitute engage

Then there's Bonnie who always has a nice smile
When we met, she was working on a craft
We were introduced again, "Have you met Bonnie?"
She also helps in the kitchen and Jim's woodcraft

There's Randy Cook with his guide dog, Shadow
And I first thought he was a student here
But it turns out he's a teacher and good at computer
He's learned a little sign which helps make him clear

Marge was my substitute teacher a few times
She knows quite a bit about different things
In cooking, she follows directions, but not me
I mix the ingredients and see what luck brings!

Betty and Marlene are teachers I didn't have
But I did get good advice from Marlene
Father Ken at St. Tom's said Betty was catechist
And I often saw Betty in the hall and kitchen

John Boes has been my counselor once again
And I'm very grateful for the help received
John, I am sure, has gone beyond the call of duty
And did his very best to get things resolved

There are many volunteers I can't forget
But there are some I never learned their names
Karen, Jim, Dot and Amy I remember best
For walking, shopping, Treat Street and games

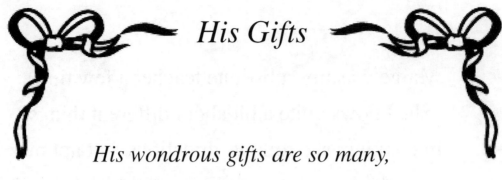

His Gifts

His wondrous gifts are so many,

Found in every nook and cranny

Seek Him, He is there, everywhere

In you and me, our Lord and Saviour

He gives us our wonderful daylight

That lasts from morn to night

His gifts are the birds and their music

And the noisy croaking frogs, so comic

In the night, are the twinkling stars

Shining on us all from Heaven afar

His gifts include the different seasons

They're ours to enjoy for many reasons

Our Lord gives love to spread and share

That all will know Him everywhere

Take His shade, coolness from the heat

Soil on which we live, Freedom's Beat

The Lord gave us friends to cherish

May His goodness shine and not perish

The Greatest Gift bestowed from above

Was the Gift of Jesus and His love

Leo Sova

Mom called tonight and gave me the sad news
    Leo Sova has gone to Heaven and will be missed
He was a true survivor of heart attacks, and all
    All who knew him were really, truly blessed

Remembering Leo is easy, he made a difference
    Always helping his fellowmen here on earth
He made the greatest homemade spaghetti sauce
    With love, a dash of time and personal worth

When disaster struck in parts of our country
    When Father Stockwell needed patio furniture
Or to raise money for Thanksgiving and Christmas
    Leo and his crew were a great fundraising mixture

Leo was an usher, sold 50/50 tickets before church
    Helped at their farm-style breakfasts for years
Leo's absolutely great fudge was a festival bestseller
    He kept going, deserving our gratitude and cheers

Leo and Hilda were married for over thirty-five years
　　And last I heard, he was teaching her to make fudge
They were special, working side by side helping others
　　Always generous, kind and loving, far as I can judge

God will give us the strength we need to continue on
　　But somehow I'll "see" Leo at the spaghetti dinners
He'll be there with encouragement for everyone to feel
　　And he can rest assured, he left behind all winners

Michigan's Potholes

It's a real shame the way the gasoline taxes go
    We can see no evidence they've fixed a pothole

Everywhere we walk, we have to be very careful
    Because Michigan's potholes are so plentiful

Governor Engler must be stashing the road money
    He's sure not helping the road repairs any

The tires go thump, bump, with a big smack
    Tempers rise and fall with all the cracks

Springtime brings a pothole contest every year
    So we show Michigan's grief and pain so clear

It's difficult enough on all those poor cars
    without the wear and tear on grocery carts

A pothole here, a pothole there, and everywhere
    All those damn potholes haven't helped anywhere

Taxpayers are tired of higher gasoline taxes
  We need to repair the highways for safety's sake

So start complaining, you working taxpayers
  Let your voices be heard, Dear Michiganders

We want to change the poor Michigan portrait
  To well kept and beautiful, not "Pothole State"

May

It's sunny May, a brand new situation
    Full of wonderment and anticipation

The days are warming unto sweet summer
    With warm breezes and fragrant flowers

The flower for the lovely month of May
    Is the sweet smelling lily of the valley

Area parades are all ready for Loyalty Day
    From our honor, let us never to stray

Sue Ann Peterson has a birthday the eighth
    She's a health aid, likes the bike path

Mother's Day is an important day set aside
    To honor mothers with love countrywide

My daughter, Tammy, was born Mother's Day
    Just seventeen minutes before Monday

Marie Calhoun lives down near the corner
    The twelfth's her birthday, I remember

The seventeenth is for my friend, Willie
   1924 to 1997 makes her seventy-three

Edith Tubbs likes a game of Scrabble
   With Evelyn Grimm, there's a double

Memorial Day is time set aside to remember
   Those folks who live in our hearts forever

Wow now, I can't forget Mary Jekel, can I?
   She was my teacher at good old Clio High

When we walk our way to town very soon now
   We'll smell the fragrant lilacs on Vienna

I remember playing with huge May beetles
   And trying not to step on little turtles

The birds are singing outside my windows
   Building nests and caring for their own

Area farmers have been out early planting
   Enjoying the dry weather we've been having

May is here, so let's enjoy it to the fullest
It will fly by and be a memory of the past

My Friend, Jill

I'm finally getting around to my friend, Jill
    It seems like forever she's been on my mind
But then I'm always running to her open door
    She's become a special friend, just my kind

Nearly three years ago, I met Harold and Jill
    Riding up the elevator at Pine Creek Manor
Then met Minnie and Elaine in the dining room
    Minnie mentioned the signing lady on my floor

I'd just moved to the manor and didn't realize
    The east and west wings had the same numbers
Minnie said this lady, Jill, lived in 313 West
    But I thought she meant me, I, well, remember

Jill Vesta Havener was born October 2nd, 1938
    The middle child of Harry and Ruth Havener
Three sisters to play with; Eva, Dorothy, Patsy
    And the youngest, Dennis, her only brother

A victim of polio at one, Jill's feet were weak
    And from Kindergarten through the fourth grade
She lived with her family around the Detroit area
    Then they returned to Clio, she's a 1956 graduate

Charles Cranstoun and Jill were wed for seven years
    They divorced and in 1979 she wed Harold Hastings
When he passed away, I became Jill's happy sidekick
    Always there helping with my poetry and pastimes

Jill learned sign language at Mott Community College
    And it's one reason I enjoy visiting her so much
I finally have someone around I can understand well
    She doesn't have to yell, but it's still a crunch

If I don't catch what she's saying, Jill accuses me
    Of not paying attention, but that's not the case
A legally blind person can't see all the movements
    And Jill can talk fast and communicate with ease

She has lived in many different parts of the country
    New Jersey in the East and California in the West
And Jill longs to visit her friends here and there
    My prayer is for her dreams to be true for the best

May 21, 1997

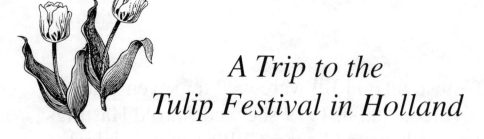

A Trip to the Tulip Festival in Holland

Happiness ruled my day when I read the Clio *Messenger*
    And I ran to Jill's apartment, her answer was yes
She would like to go to the Tulip Festival in Holland
    I called Rose, a friend from Holland, we made plans

The day, May 14th, was a typical "Michigan Weather" day
    As we left Clio by motorcoach at 7:30 in the morn
Ann had orange and apple juice and donut holes for all
    Our driver did fine, and we arrived well before noon

Luncheon was served at Evergreen Commons Senior Center
    Meatloaf, mashed potatoes and strawberry shortcake
This grandma bought some postcards and a little puzzle
    And missed the show for no one's place wanted to take

Ann thought a good place to meet Rose was at the parade
    But Rose couldn't find a driver, so didn't make it
The parade was marching bands, the Dutch, and old cars
    The rain held off and that made a fantastic hit

The tulips were beautiful red, purple, pink, yellow
    And a Dutch play we saw at Holland Christian School
Jill and I sat in back and I could hear the nice music
    I was later told the dancing was in wooden shoes

They served a delicious dinner before we headed home
    Of chicken, rice, jello, vegetables and ice cream
We started for home and all agreed the day was great
    The rain poured all the way, I watched it stream

Ann had bingo to play; Jill played but I was too tired
    However, I could hear Ann, she had a very good voice
Some acquaintances I knew from this crowd on our trip
    Besides Jill were Irma, Brenda, also John and Alice

I called Rose the next morning and there's a big fine
    If you pick a tulip in Holland, I never picked any
Michigan weather is unpredictable, no one minded much
    And I think everyone enjoyed their trip away

May 23, 1997

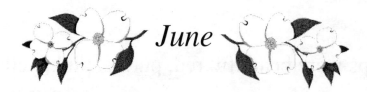

June

After a cool, rainy May, I can't believe June's here
   Most of us are hoping for a real summer this year

Pepper, a service dog, is owned by Anders Hustvedt
   I see Anders celebrates his birthday the second

Dorothy Grai, I've met for just a few short visits
   She gets Communion via Catholic Christian Services

Her birthday's the seventh, same as my elder daughter
   Melinda'll be thirty, we're celebrating with dinner

A note of memory is due Herbie Lawrence on June tenth
   He was a good checkers player and fighter, the truth

Bea Moret, a real sweetheart, makes beautiful afghans
   She lives under us in 213 East and never complains

I remember the beautiful roses we had on Roseberry
   White, yellow, red and pink; they bloomed yearly

The second whole week in June is "National Hug Week"
   So spread those arms for the biggest super squeeze

The fourteenth is a day set aside to honor our flag
   Let it ever to wave, a symbol of truth and brave

We must remember our wonderful fathers everywhere
   For where would we be without them to deeply care?

For Erma Boling, the nineteenth is her special day
   She exercises and joins us for euchre on Saturday

Should I say the twenty-first is the start of summer?
   It's beyond thinking with the crazy Michigan weather

The twenty-second of June is for my youngest grandson
   He'll be one, two, THREE; is Grandma right, Brandon?

Of course, I would never forget our very own Pat Atkin
   The last of June's her day, she's in our office plan

Believe me, I don't know where the time's gone so far
   But June has come fast and it's the halfway mark

We have to try and grasp the moment, it fleeting goes
   It's here and gone, sweet memories, everyone knows

June has always been one of my favorite months to play
   Outside and jump around in the sweet fragrant hay

Melinda

I graduated, got married and had a cute baby girl

   Born Wednesday, June 7th, 1967, a hot sunny day

And weighing in at seven pounds and seven ounces

   We named her Melinda Lou, hoping sweet and gay

Melinda took her first steps alone at twelve months

   Christmas 1968 found her sick with encephalitis

She spent nearly five months at McLaren Hospital

   Undergoing physical therapy to help through this

Early Christmas morning, when she was a curious four

   I found her opening all the gifts beneath the tree

At five she started kindergarten at Durrant-Tuuri-Mott

   Taking sign language lessons from Mrs. Helen Tardy

Then Mel and I had to take sign language classes also

They were offered free at Flint Southwestern High

And a whole new experience opened before our very eyes

Helping us talk to the deaf, also between Mel and I

In 1977 when Melinda was ten, she was poster child

For The Genesee County United Way Organization

She and "Big Sister" Rose were on TV commercials

With the sunset behind them, a lovely situation

Melinda graduated from Michigan School for the Deaf

Then went to work at Flint's Community Industries

She had a history of falling when walking or riding

And seemed to desire ambulances and emergencies

Melinda scorned Seminole living quarter guidelines

   And moved to New York Avenue with three deaf men

One, Randy, fell head over heels in love with her

   They fixed up a house on Church Street, their own

Lloyd (Randy) Kammers, Jr. has become special to us

   He worked as a window installer for eighteen years

His brothers and sister all learned sign language

   Our family is happy Melinda has found someone dear

Well, 1997 is here and although it can't be possible

   It's twenty years since Melinda was a poster child

And eleven years have come and gone since graduation

   Yes, I am a proud Mom to a thirty-year-old child

May 28, 1997

The Gift of a Child

A child is a gift from the Lord above
   The child is yours to nurture and love
To raise him with the very best of care
   To teach him to play, work and share
The child is so precious because he's yours
   but then after all those beautiful hours
Of raising our children in the Right Way
   They are supposed to leave, not to stay
But some of our children are handicapped
   The Lord loves them too, and at home kept
The Lord loves all children, great and small
   And wants us to raise them to stand tall

October 20, 1997

My Troubles Tonight

I have no idea what's the matter with me
I lay down to sleep, but I'm not, you see

My ears hurt and my feet won't stop itching
And I'm finding this situation bewitching

My head can't stop its ceaseless thinking
To my tiredness all day, I'll be sinking

I think of Melinda so fast approaching thirty
And knowing this is also my year to be fifty

No, I'm not afraid, that's just not the case
Because the Lord is there with me always

I put some Avon lotion on my feet a bit ago
　　But they still itch like a repeating echo

So, what on earth are these problems tonight?
　　I lay to sleep but toss and turn all night

This writing can be a thorn in my poor heart
　　The aching and longing stay, never to part

Lord, I wanted my precious Mel beside me
　　always
　　　　But the past is sweet memories, these are
　　　　today's

So, I'll try again to rest and sleep in peace
　　And know I've written another feeling piece

June 2, 1997

205

Senior Power Day at Crossroads

Rain, rain, rain, also cold and miserable
   That's the best description I can figure
Of "Senior Power Day" at Crossroads Village
   But we were in a tent, away from nature

    Melinda, Randy, Alice and I stayed together
      And we had two wheelchairs between us four
    They were meant to be for Alice and Melinda
      But Alice took me through the muddy tour

There was a group of Flint Deaf Club members
   And interpreters so they could join the fun
It was a free day with lunch and ride for all
   Then out in the muddy ruts we'd try to run

    To get to the bathroom, we sloshed through mud
      And it seemed to rain harder all the way.
    Lunch was good; chicken, potato salad, beans
      And bingo in the afternoon ended the day

There were several folks I knew from the area
    Ann Anderson, our leader, Bernadine Callahan
Dale Hyde, Ruth Bully, Francis and Doris O'Hearn
    There were others but out of my mind they ran

        We four who went to the library in Randy's car
            Decided to take a ride on the merry-go-round
        Randy and Melinda rode in a seat built for two
            Alice and I rode horses; round, up and down

Well, what could you expect from Mother Nature
    If everything is planned for a warm, sunny day?
She's full of jokes, it's best to be prepared
    We were pretty much and enjoyed our stay...

People

People are as different as night and day
   Some are so sad, while others are happy
Some like to dance, sing and merrily play
   while we wonder why others are snappy

Some folks are secure, while others worry
   There are night owls who sleep all day
And those who are always in a big hurry
   Some are talkers, others have naught to say

There are clowns who enjoy making others laugh
   Some folks you can depend on to volunteer
Others are leaders at the head of the staff
   Still others are followers, far or near

Some people are smart, some are friendly
   Some of us stay short while some get tall
Some are complainers, while others are silly
   One thing for sure, the Lord made us all

We are all handicapped to a certain degree
No one can possibly know everything
There's the lame, deaf and those who can't
A stunning variety, interesting making

God made all of His people different, unique
Therefore, you can be sure He loves us all
There's no two people quite exactly alike
We are all His people, the great and small

A Birthday to Remember

Hard to believe Melinda was approaching thirty
   She called and said she wanted to celebrate
I gave Tammy a call, we put our ideas together
   And decided on a boat ride and dinner date

Amy's Little Signs had clocks in sign language
   At Deaf Expo '96 in Los Angeles, California
And I'm glad I brought an advertisement home
   As it made a nice birthday gift for Melinda

Everyone likes surprises and Melinda does too
   So we decided we'd get together for dinner
On June first or eighth at Applebee's Restaurant
   The first of June was cold, eighth was better

Melinda and her sweetheart were kept in the dark
   About why we wished for a nice, warm, sunny day
Everyone agreed the meal at Applebee's was great
   And then our little family secret we gave away

There was room on the boat for all nine celebrants
    Melinda and Randy, Tammy and Brian, and Michael
My son, Brian, and grandsons, Joshua and Brandon
    That's eight, the ninth is this writer, as well

With a huge splash, the beautiful boat took off
    Captain Brian Burt was navigator on fast runs
Making her splash cold spray as she sped along
    And Melinda, Joshua and Brandon all had turns

We picked a wonderful day, dinner was delicious
    Everyone loved the boat ride in the nice weather
Melinda liked the sign clock and crystal flutes
    Now she's thirty and has a birthday to remember

I could "hear" those high waves singing to her
    "Happy birthday to you. Happy thirtieth, Melinda"

July

Summer came in the beautiful month of June
    And the birds sang their sweetest tune

Now, it's July and half the year has flown
    Though it seems like yesterday it began

Today is special for two dear people I know
    Tammy and Brian; nine years continue to grow

Two hundred and twenty-one years have passed
    Since July 4, 1776, when freedom was declared

Dave Clase, our maintenance man, is special
    Always busy, we see him everyday in the hall

July fourteenth is a birthday for Hazel Taylor
    She's the little woman who lives next door

Also, on the fourteenth, at two in the afternoon
    The Dauner Dollies will be here to play a tune

On July seventeenth my grandson, Josh'll be five
    Old enough to start kindergarten, sakes alive!

A nice lady across from the elevator does abide
    The 18th is her day, the name is Winona McBride

Elaine Stewart is fondly remembered in this poem
    She'd sit at our table, the west wing her home

My dear Mel died the twentieth, a hot day in July
    It's been six years now, memories of a nice guy

Happy Birthday to Paula Shaw, our Manor manager
    She works in the office making things better

My sister, Karen, is also missed by her family
    Our Lord took her Home four years ago this July

I'd hate to think I could ever forget Janet and Gary
    The twenty-sixth marks their fifth anniversary

A notice this week said Brett Doyle is leaving
    He is one more person we'll all be missing

July is raspberry ripening and picking time
    They're my favorite to put in a summer pie

Sure hope we all enjoy the lovely month of July
    Once it's gone, on its memories we'll rely

July 1, 1997

Deaf–Blind Camp
June 20–22, 1997

I asked Michelle from the Visually Impaired Center
    About going to a deaf camp, then later in April
I received an invitation to a deaf-blind workshop
    There was a limit, so I replied back by first mail

Then later in May, with some openings still left
    I asked my friend, Joan, if she'd like to join us
And her answer was "yes," that made it extra special
    Once again, we'd be roommates, a wonderful plus

Deb Wright and her dog, Chelsea, completed our room
    So we were ready for the fourth weekend in June
Julie picked up Joan and me on a rainy afternoon
    They had spaghetti ready, so we weren't too soon

After dinner, there was a meeting to get acquainted
    And I met some very nice folks that rainy night
A few folks were there for a crash course in ASL
    And to teach them, Joan and I thought a delight

We went on a starry pontoon boat ride on Vineyard Lake
    And we stayed awake late talking and signing away
Maureen, from Detroit, interpreted for Joan and me
    Before we left for bed, she said she couldn't stay

Saturday was very busy from early morning until night
    First breakfast, then meetings about different ways
There were to help the deaf and blind community
    Everyone was so nice and well organized always

We had a choice of activities to do for the afternoon
    Three boat rides; speed, pontoon and paddle boat
Also, swimming, water skiing and horseback riding
    We had helpers and life jackets to keep us afloat

Those of us folks who desired went to Mass at five
    In a tiny, little church; The Sacred Heart of Jesus
There were interpreters for all who asked for them
    The priest knew sign and signed the Mass for us

I met Phyllis Genna before the final Saturday meeting
    She's a real sweetheart, as Dee had described her
Trying to make her understand me was my undoing and
    My loud voice kept others from hearing the speaker

Breakfast Sunday morning, then one last, long meeting
    My eyes so wearily watching the interpreters hands
The meeting was held in the little Catholic church
    We were all together there, united as good friends

Dee Robertson, Cindy and the rest of the organizers
    Did a fabulous job of helping the deaf and blind
No one was ever left out or forgotten in the crowd
    The weekend was a lovely experience to all inclined

July 7, 1997

September Fest '97

September 5th, 6th and 7th is our festival

    And we'd like to invite you, one and all

Bring the entire family and join the fun

    Maybe you'd enjoy the Saturday Road Run

There are horseshoe and volleyball tournaments

    And don't forget to browse through the tents

You'll find baked goods, arts and crafts

    Who knows, maybe a few Christmas gifts

Be sure and bring the kids to the games tent

    Where they can play to their heart's content

We also have a special tent for next to new

    Take a look, maybe there's something for you

Everyone seems to have a stomach for spaghetti

    And the ushers will be serving you on Friday

Saturday's dinner is going to be Swiss Steak

    Bar-B-Q Chicken on Sunday tops the cake

There'll be a special place for bingo

    And if you like gambling, there's casino

Take a break if you get tired or hungry

    Food booths and picnic tables are ready

You'll find elephant ears, popcorn, hot dogs

    Also, French fries, pizza, pop and nachos

We have the Sunday night $10,000 raffle

    You could be the winner in the big shuffle

There'll be clowns to bring cheer to everyone

    And music will continue all weekend long

This festival is at Saints Charles and Helena

    In the middle of Clio, at 230 East Vienna

So come one, come all and join the family fun

    Cuz our festival has something for everyone

August

I just cannot believe how fast summer's flying
It just doesn't seem possible August is coming

I saw Francis Scott Key on my manor calendar
Remember he wrote "The Star Spangled Banner"

A true sweetheart has her birthday the third
Her name's Minnie Eisinger, spread the word

Minnie has to share her day with Martha Lenk
Who has a first floor apartment, west wing

Joe and Jane Vincent both have August birthdays
A nice couple, sure hope they have super days

The fourteenth is reserved for our own Mary Gadany
This is extra special because she's sweet fifty

To a sweet little lady, it's August twenty-first
It's Georgia Kitson and it must be eighty-first

There is a birthday the same day for Ed Misener
He's new to our community here at the manor

Someone who lives here is fast approaching fifty
Oh dear, it just can't be, but it is. I'm guilty

August thirtieth's for a nice lady, Leona Frammolino
Her last name makes me think of a lovely flamingo

You know, I just remembered, I left out Mona Bruff
I hope I'm forgiven cuz I can't be in the rough

Her birthday is the sixteenth of this lovely month
I feel better now. She gets two verses for youth

Born the end of August, Mildred Knox likes euchre
And plays with the folks at the Clio Senior Center

To children everywhere August is the end of summer
Soon there'll be "Back to School" sales all over

This farmer's daughter remembers summer's labor
And yesterday's distance from neighbor to neighbor

I recall the excitement of returning to school
With a desire to learn and to try the rules

July 29, 1997

Dear Lynn and Alna

My heart and my thinking are running in poetry

    So I'll write a poem for your anniversary

Many things have changed since you said "I do"

    And I'll try to name just a few for you

Fifty years ago, more people lived on farms

    Won friendship with decent homespun charms

There were a lot more woods around to explore

    We grew up helping with every little chore

There weren't computers back then with answers

    To all the little wishes the heart desires

Visiting friends and neighbors was a classic

    Reading, writing and arithmetic were basic

There was more land distance between neighbors

    But many things were shared, including labors

Horses, buggies and Model T's roamed the streets

There were no air conditioners or seat belts

A lot of roads weren't paved and had ruts yearly

For which the horses and carriages paid dearly

We didn't need the cops at school way back then

If the rules were broken, you felt it behind

There's still love and caring for our fellowman

In bad situations, they'll lend a helping hand

I'm wishing you the very best for your golden day

And may you be blessed with happiness always

Happy 50th anniversary to you both

September

I'll swear the year just got started yesterday
But my calendar tells me today is Labor Day

The summer has flown by fast on eagle's wings
September's here, we'll see what fall brings

John Kertesz's birthday is eighth of September
From the west wing, he puts puzzles together

Another birthday is the eighth of September
Eunice Hustvedt, I see her often with Pepper

Glenna Harris enjoys the dining room company
She sells Avon, the eleventh is her birthday

Violet Baker is the nice lady across the hall
She's seventy-five, in my book, that's tall

Today I looked at my calendar, it's the twelfth
It's no longer Labor Day, time just moves forth

September's Festival is the beauty of nature
When golds, reds and browns make the picture

Hazel Bridges is from next door, the little lady
I got her mixed up with Hazel Taylor in July

Rainy, cool days are a sure sign fall is here
Soon falling leaves will leave the trees bare

Dad's eighty-second falls on Good Neighbor Day
A fitting tribute to a fine man, I must say

It's time for harvest and to prepare for winter
Thank the Lord, there's time before December

October

Here I go again, yesterday was September's end
And today is the first of October, my friend

I see Lloyd Empey often down checking his mail
His birthday's today, I hope it's very special

Tomorrow is the seventy-eighth for John Calhoun
He stands at Clio square looking around town

Her day's tomorrow, she is on my mind all year
I just can't forget Jill Hastings, so dear

For two darling folks, John and Alice Kertesz
October fifth marks fifty-four anniversaries

Two Margarets have October birthdays from the Manor
Margaret Key and Margaret Johnson, I know neither

Christopher Columbus discovered America in 1492
I'm glad he took that chance voyage, aren't you?

No finer folks do I know than my dear mom and dad
Love still shines and fifty-two years they've had

Mystery and romance are favorites of Winnie Sherman
The twenty-fourth it is, should be a great one

A nice man, Bill Harris, enjoys doing jigsaw puzzles
His day's in October, close to ghosts and goblins

The thirty-first and last of October is Halloween
Witches, ghosts, goblins and black cats are seen

October is the month when lovely autumn is on parade
Golds, reds, yellows, to summer a farewell is bade

Smells of burning leaves, sweet memos of yesteryear
And searching the attic for old Halloween gear

A Trip to Nashville, September, 1997

We packed our things, some melon and bananas
   With expectations for a good time in Tennessee
Dad, Mom, Shirley, Janet and I were all going
   And Janet drove the eight hundred mile journey

Despite a detour, rain and bad windshield wiper
   We made it to Nashville in good time Wednesday
Checked into the Clubhouse Inn, our destination
   And I saw Jimmy Blessington first on Thursday

Nashville has some interesting tours, we made plans
   For a bus tour, that's when Al Calvi joined us
We toured a wax museum of life-size famous singers
   Then planned for a dinner and dance, but no bus

So Al and Jimmy got us sisters tickets for dinner
   We ate and talked and I gave them some poetry
Where, oh where had Mom and Dad disappeared to?
   They'd gone to the army party room for company

Friday afternoon found us on a historical tour
  Of Ryman Auditorium, a century old music hall
And Andrew Jackson's home with the highest beds
  The Grand Ole Opry I missed, but wrote to Neal

Saturday we saw the old cars of the music stars
  And went on a boat ride on the Cumberland River
The boat holds 1,200 people and they serve lunch
  Autumn was on parade, a calm beautiful wonder

Six of us went to Mass in a 150 year-old landmark
  St. Mary's of the Seven Sorrows Catholic Church
Then the reason for coming to the Music City, USA
  The army reunion party with a dinner-dance touch

Jimmy was staying until Monday and asked us to stay
  The decision was ours, it depended on the weather
Beautiful Sunday, we went to Opryland Theme Park
  Where music shows made me long for an interpreter

Then a show of wonder and beauty at Opryland Hotel
 Which is built with four sides, its middle domed
Sofa red, blue, yellow and green lights, on and off
 The floater danced and swayed as the music flowed

I'll remember most two special guys on this trip
 And how I longed to join in their conversation
Jimmy Blessington and Al Calvi, the precious two
 Who gave the three Karner girls a fun vacation

There's also Surgee, Joe, Betty, Donna and Verna
 There's the folks from Rhode Island, Pete and Sis
The next reunion will be in Jefferson City, Missouri
 We're planning for a good time, we don't want to miss

Life

Life is much too short for grudges

    Too precious for senseless smudges

It's too wonderful for nasty gossip

    That tears from the speaker's lip

Life is a wondrous gift from our Lord

    And to ruin it, we can't afford

A full life can be the happiest thing

    To make us want to dance and sing

The material things that money buys

    Like mansions and expensive toys

Are not what makes for true happiness

    It's self-respect and real gladness

Life is chock full of ups and downs

    How they're mastered is what counts

If through kindnesses, we bring smiles

    Then it must be worth the extra miles

It's the little things that most matter

    The free gestures that make life better

A smile, a hug, some special kindnesses

    Sharing and driving away loneliness

Life is enjoying God's beautiful treasures

    And getting the most from little pleasures

November 1, 1997

For a Scrabble Game

Who'll be my friendly opponents in Scrabble today

　A game for over thirty years, I've loved to play?

I wonder who'll it be; Tom, Olive, Ruth or Vivian

　Or could it be Chuck, Ida Mae, Neal or Lillian?

What fun it is to make words one way at a stretch

　and see how many different words we can fetch

Since seeing the ad in January's *Flint Journal*

　I played with Mary Ellen, then joined in April

Good players, they give me lots of competition

　With two and three letter words and intention

Words to use the "Q" without needing a single "U"

　Now that could just be competition enough for you

A good thing we are allowed to use a dictionary

　Cuz our brains could explode with the memory

As sure as words rhyme, I love a Scrabble round

So many a Tuesday, that's where I'll be found.

Where the competition is, my excitement's a word

Or two or three to see just how much I've scored

I'm happy to be in the Scrabble club with Vivian

Olive, Tom, Chuck, Ruth, Ida Mae, Neal and Lillian

And so thankful for the gift of oversized letters

A big help, and I can see to play so much better

Scrabble

November

Well, here it's almost the middle of November

Somehow time is getting lost to me forever.

I noticed Helen Glass is written for November

but I fear a mistake for it was in October

Lois Barrington had her birthday on the third

And Frances Roy the fifth, friends, I heard

Our war veterans were honored on the eleventh

For America they fought, giving her strength

November nineteenth is a date for Maxine George

She enjoys thirty-one with Marie and George

Alice Dysvick went with us on Senior Power Day

    We had fun, sure hope she has a nice birthday

Frances Roy, Lois Barrington and Alice Dysvick

    Friends side-by-side, first floor, west wing

Thanksgiving is the fourth Thursday in November

    America gives thanks today, tomorrow, forever

Of course, the twenty-eighth is Walt Labrenz's

    He rhymes with November's birthstone, topaz

Snow fell on Veteran's Day, so white and pretty

    The first snowfalls thick enough for me to see

November is getting very close to the year's end

    Colder days and snow are forecast, my friend

December

Believe it or not, next month is December
What in the world happened to November?

Margaret Smith lives on the second floor
East wing and I see her in the elevator

My son, Brian, was born on December fifth
And this year marks his twenty-seventh

I know Pat Grant who lives across the hall
Her ceiling's the one that had a great fall

Pat Grant's special day is December tenth
She can use some prayers for good health

I don't know if I know Bessie Dasen, do I?
She has a birthday the twelfth, oh my

Also on December twelfth is Allen Battles
At the end of the west wing he settles

My dear mom was born December thirteenth
  Extra special, this is seventy-fifth

Just down the hall live Joe and Jane Vincent
  Fifty-two years the fourteenth, I knew it

BRRR The twenty-first winter is starting
  I admit, I'm looking forward to spring

Mr. and Mrs. G. Hollenback have been together
  Forty-six years on twenty-third of December

The birth of our Lord, Jesus, is Christmas
  Let us rejoice and happily sing to Jesus

New Year's Eve is the final day of the year
  May His blessings rain on all far and near

Another Birthday to Remember

I thought I'd write this August twenty-seventh
    Which was the very last day I was forty-nine
And I thought of it also on the twenty-eighth
    The day I turned fifty, but today seems fine

Randy and Melinda were out the week before
    And before they left said, "See you Sunday"
What was going to happen then, I wasn't sure
    My family had planned a surprise birthday

The pictures were ready, the family and guests
    A beautiful birthday cake sat amid the snacks
Balloons filled the dining room with good wishes
    "Over the hill," was wrapped on a table in back

The surprise party was set for the twenty-fourth
    All the arrangements had been made in secret
My being in Indiana helped for what it's worth
    Making it easy to come and my address book get

Among the guests at the party Sunday afternoon
    Were Randy and Melinda, Fred and JoAnn LaHale
Dave, Sharon, Brian, Tammy, Joshua and Brandon
    Shirley, Greg, Scott, Kelly and my friend, Neal

Mom and Dad, also Jack and Darlene Emmendorfer
    Janet and Gary, Fred, Willie and Bob Eickholt
Leonard Walther and his boys, and Carol Waner
    George and Mildred Hollenback, Alice Dysvick

My son, Brian, Jill Hastings and Dorothy King
    My brother, Larry, Jennifer, Kevin and Lindsay
Also among the guests in the dining room gathering
    Were my niece, Carrie, and her daughter, Ashley

The dining room was bursting with all the dears
    But there were friends who couldn't be there
Ron and Karen Stanbaugh, friends of twenty years
    Joan Krauss, Sandy Carsten and Joyce, her mother

That lovely cake had a book titled, "Patty's Poems"
    My family gave me a beautiful oak plate holder
And I had some budding roses hanging in my home
    This special day just for me, I'll remember

— November 27, 1997 —

Libraries

Libraries are such quiet places
    Such wonderful places to think
There's computer and table spaces
    Where we can write down anything

    Libraries are full of "golden" opportunity
       Good knowledge, useful through the ages
    References, copyrights, whatever's necessary
       The answers are there in millions of pages

There's no comparison to going to the library
    Maybe we'll go to browse in its quietness
Or to find a good western or book of mystery
    And I'm writing this poem amid its stillness

There's many different books to read

History, mystery, math or biology

There's English books to help proceed

In the wonderful world of knowledge

The library has a section for little folks

With every kind of book for learning

And tells them colors from reds to purples

When they grow, how to start earning

Sometimes, there's a few noisy computers

With their keys busily ticking away

They're full of lists and word processors

That can be a big help from day to day

Winter Memories

No more green leaves against the blue sky
    The children weren't playing in the pools
Yesterday was so very cold, bleak and cloudy
    And children had switched to their wools

During the night, I peeked out the window
    And discovered the earth was transformed
God had brightened the landscape with snow
With thoughts of cold, wintry days reborn

I thought of building a long ago snow fort
    Of slipping, sliding and falling on ice
Back then the farmhouse was heated by wood
    Dad got the wood and stoked the furnace

The roads were icy and danger lurked there
    Strangers on Hurd went right in the ditch
Cuz they couldn't make the curve by a hair
    And Uncle John helped with a tractor hitch

I remember spreading our arms and legs wide
    And making angels in the soft fresh snow
On cold winter days, the cows stayed inside
    And ate grain and hay stored up in the mow

I've never liked four or five foot snowdrifts
    Cuz they tend to bewilder my weakened eyes
It's hard telling if the snow's in a big drift
    So stumble and grumble do I with huge sighs

There was the year drifts filled up Elmsdale
    I was a young mom and Tammy left for school
But back on Elmsdale, the bus did a big stall
    Got stuck, couldn't go and to kids how cool

    Fresh winter snow can sparkle like diamonds
        Ice looks like glass hanging from the eaves
        Christmas glitter brightens the world around
        No matter, I look for spring and new leaves

Some days I am not sure it's December
    And I'm sure Mother Nature isn't either

She can't make up her mind what to do
    Should spring be here, or should it snow?

Still there are signs December's here
    Goodwill is being spread everywhere

Christmas lights are glittering brightly
    Yuletide carols can be heard nightly

Santa and his elves have been so busy
    Working and there's no time to be lazy

People hoped for a nice white Christmas
    But we saw last summer's sodden grass

My calendar says we're near year's end
    Are there any wrongs we have to mend?

Now, I'm not sure if sense I should make
    And trying to think makes my head ache

Writing is what I enjoy, so write I will
    The new year'll bring more of it still

We should make a new year's resolution
    And make the most of our good intention

Love and prayer, ask the Lord to steer
    Clink the glass and ring in the new year

As 1997 bows out with its many memories
    We welcome 1998 with brand new stories

Happy New Year wishes go out to one and all
    From this author just down the east hall

Nineteen Ninety-Seven

Nineteen ninety-seven has flown and gone
  A new year, nineteen ninety-eight has begun

The last year has left its many memories
  Some good, some bad, but all have stories

A car backed into me in the middle of February
  The pain in my hip causing me much worry

My oldest daughter, Melinda, turned thirty
  And I left behind my forties, I'm fifty

Five times I visited Crossroads Village
  And twice went on a horse drawn carriage

I just keep thinking about the many sounds
  And no one keeps me off the merry-go-rounds

Someone very special entered my life in June
  And we started singing our own new tune

The I-75 and M-57 project was finally begun
  But there's question if it'll ever be done

Patty's Poems was turned down by one press
  But neither do I have despair nor distress

I enjoyed a weekend at Vineyard Lake in June
   And a boat ride under the stars and moon

Our Thetford Township had a tornado in July
   BOOM CRASH BANG, we heard thunder's reply

My grandson, Josh, now goes to kindergarten
   He taught this grandma a little sign lesson

My little grandsons are growing very fast
   Better watch or childhood's days will be past

My daughter, Tammy, graduated from college
   A mother, a wife and a lot of work, I allege

These memories aren't necessarily in order
   I am just jotting them down as I remember

Life wouldn't be life if everything's perfect
   So we've got to take it like it is, imperfect

The year, nineteen ninety-eight, is here now
   We better enjoy it for it'll be gone tomorrow

In Conclusion

I have really enjoyed writing this book

And hope you'll do better than look

These pages are full of my heart and soul

Often they have made me swear and growl

Because of the many mistakes I have made

I feel my debt to my Master has been paid

I peer through my magnifier for the way

With never a thought of giving up today

This is a dream I've dreamed for so long

Now it is time to sing my success song

With my sensor, a true poet I can be

It's not easy cuz these words I can't see

But there are many good memories to write

I'll do another book with all my might

I love to make words and meaning rhyme

And will do my very best every time

With love and best wishes to my family

Friends and fans, the best is yet to be

January 8, 1998

A Little About Myself ---

I am proud to be a farmer's daughter
    And the name is Patricia Mae Karner
At five, I was sick with encephalitis
    That badly affected my ears and eyes

My life has centered in Clio, Michigan
    I've left on vacations and back again
Clio has changed a lot in fifty years
    Since we raised hens, pigs and steers

Shirley, me, Janet, Larry and Karen
    Made up the five Karner children
We all loved little pups and kitties
    Playing in the mow and in the trees

Mom and Dad still live on their farm
    With its old-fashioned country charm
I have always loved to work and play
    And enjoyed rides on the fresh hay

In 1966, Malcolm Grindel and I wed
    And with three little ones blessed
Some of my poetry is about my friends
    And there's a lot about odds and ends

— April 22, 1998 —